CHARLES JOHN HEXAMER
*President of the National German-American
Alliance, 1901–1917*

THE GERMAN- AMERICANS IN POLITICS
1914–1917

CLIFTON JAMES CHILD

THE UNIVERSITY OF WISCONSIN PRESS
MADISON

Printed in the United States of America

PREFACE

THIS IS A STUDY OF ONE OF THE LARGE RACIAL GROUPS OF THE United States during years that were critical for that group, as they were for the nation as a whole. Exactly *how* critical, there is no need to demonstrate here. The book is concerned merely with the group as such, with its reactions to the war in Europe and to neutrality at home, its political activities and their relation to wider national issues, its possibly conflicting loyalties, and its vicissitudes in the face of the growing resentment and intolerance of other sections of the community. There is no underlying claim that the Germans have played a more significant role, in proportion to their numbers, than any other element in American history, and no conscious attempt is made to give them more limelight than they deserve.

The author, who is a citizen of Great Britain, became imbued with a desire to learn more of the Germans in the United States, in the first instance, through a deep acquaintance with the life and culture of their European fatherland. That desire was subsequently gratified by the award of a Commonwealth Fund Fellowship, which enabled him to spend two years at the University of Wisconsin in 1936–1938; this is, it may be added, only one of several ways in which he feels himself indebted to the generosity of the Fund and the kindness of its officers.

It was his privilege to undertake his research in the American history seminar of Professor John D. Hicks. From him he received the guidance and encouragement, the sympathy and understanding, that made his task in every way a happy, as well as a fruitful one.

He is indebted further to Mr. Siegmund G. von Bosse, formerly president of the National German-American Alliance, for reading and suggesting revisions in his manuscript and for cooperating willingly at every stage; to Dr. John A. Hawgood of the University of Birmingham, England, for suggestions and help with the reading of proofs; to Miss Marjorie J. Morse for assistance with the typescript; to the editor of the *Mississippi Valley Historical Review* for permission to reprint in Chapter III material already published in that journal; to Messrs. Siegmund G. and Georg von Bosse, Miss E. Niedner, and the editor of the *New Yorker Herold und Staats-Zeitung* for permission to use the illustrations accompanying the text; and to various German-American leaders and others, too numerous to mention by name, who have granted interviews and supplied information during the course of the research.

CLIFTON JAMES CHILD

Birmingham, England
August 1939

CONTENTS

ILLUSTRATIONS

I

PAN–GERMANS AND AMERICAN–GERMANS

WHEN WAR BROKE OUT IN EUROPE IN 1914, AMERICANS who were actively hostile to Germany found themselves confronted with a powerful and well-organized movement of their fellow citizens of German descent. While by no means unanimous in their view of the international situation, the German-Americans stood together in numbers sufficient to make it clear that their feelings might play an important part in national affairs while the crisis lasted. Disconcerting as this situation was, it seemed easily explicable. To those of pro-Ally sympathies there was little doubt that the agents of German expansionism, so loudly denounced in the Allied press at the beginning of the war, had laid their plans in this country likewise. The German Empire, it was to be assumed, in line with its *Weltpolitik* of the past thirty years, had welded the German-Americans together into a bloc favorable to its scheme of world domination. The United States, untutored in the subtleties of such intrigues, had fallen a victim to Pan-Germanism. The hand of the Teutonic schemer had tampered with its politics. Its public life had become tainted with *Kultur*—a word terrible to those whose ignorance of the language obscured from them the fact that it at least meant both "culture" and "civilization."

Was not the sinister form of the conspiracy clearly suggested by the remarkable readiness with which the German-American organizations sprang to the defense of the fatherland against its American critics? And by the flourishing German-language press? And by the general tendency, in German-American communities, to favor German, even in preference to English, as the medium of instruction in the public schools?

According to one writer, there was "nothing in this country which would offer an excuse for this movement. Its main-springs must be found elsewhere."[1] The German-Americans must be conforming to designs of German origin. Even so well-informed a student of international affairs as William Roscoe Thayer, in writing his biography of John Hay in the early months of the war, was led away for a moment from his general theme to reflect that "under the pretense of pro-moting political and commercial friendship, the German Government began secretly to organize the German-Ameri-cans. Agents of all kinds were sent out from Germany and the German-Americans, who had been looked at rather as absconders by the Imperial Government, were now flattered, courted and encouraged in all ways to renew their intimacy with the Fatherland and to regard it as their real home."[2]

Any anti-German writer indeed who could ignore for a moment the chronic disfavor which the Pan-Germans had met from their government[3] might argue speciously that their aspirations had been fostered by that government or its agents among the German element in the United States. Back in 1899, only a few years after the foundation of the Pan-German Union in Berlin, the various German-American societies and clubs of Pennsylvania had federated into a German-American Central Alliance. For president they had chosen Dr. Charles John Hexamer, the son of a distinguished Forty-Eighter, and a prosperous civil engineer of Phila-delphia. In collaboration with the new secretary, Adolph Timm, a native of Posen, Hexamer began to work out a

[1] Gustavus Ohlinger, *Their True Faith and Allegiance* (Macmillan, New York, 1916), 42. See also André Cheradame, *The United States and Pan-Germania* (Scribners, New York, 1918).

[2] *Life and Letters of John Hay* (2 vols., Houghton Mifflin, Boston and New York, 1915), 2:277–278.

[3] Bülow, for example, expresses contempt for the Pan-Germans. See his *Memoirs* (Little, Brown, Boston, 1931), 2:253–254. They were the cause of some embarrassment to more than one German chancellor.

scheme for a national federation of all German-American organizations, and on October 6, 1901, he summoned a convention of representatives from Pennsylvania, Maryland, Ohio, New York, New Jersey, Missouri, Wisconsin, and Minnesota, to meet in the hall of the German Society at Philadelphia. This convention resulted in the formation of the National German-American Alliance, of which Hexamer and Timm became president and secretary.[4]

The object of the Alliance, as defined in the constitution which it adopted, was to bring together citizens of German descent for the pursuit of "such just aspirations and interests as are not inconsistent with the general weal of the country and the rights and duties of good citizens; for the protection of the German element against 'nativistic' attacks [*that is, against the activities of the prohibitionists*]; and for the promotion of sound, amicable relations between America and the old German fatherland." Its program was primarily cultural. Use of the German tongue was to be fostered in the public schools in all districts where the German element was strong, "upon the following broad principle that, next to the English, the German language has become one of universal use." Physical training, on the lines of the old *Turner* movement, was to be made part of the American educational system. Attention was to be given to the German contribution to American history.[5] Finally, the Alliance would call upon "all Germans to gain their citizenship as soon as they were legally entitled to it; to take an active interest in public affairs; and to practice their civic duty, with regard to the ballot box, fearlessly and according to their own consciences."[6]

---

[4] The German title adopted by the organization was *Der Deutschamerikanische Nationalbund*. See *Das Buch der Deutschen in Amerika*, edited by Max Heinrici (National German-American Alliance, Philadelphia, 1909), 781, 783–784; *Americana Germanica*, edited by Marion D. Learned (New York, 1902), 4: 207–208; and *Denkschrift*, issued by the Executive Committee of the National Alliance, in *German-American Annals* (continuation of *Americana Germanica*, 1903), 1:491–492.

[5] The Missouri Alliance, for example, subsequently published at Sedalia a historical quarterly entitled *Deutsche Geschichtsforschung für Missouri*.

[6] Constitution of the Alliance, in Heinrici, *Das Buch der Deutschen*, 781, 782.

This was the beginning of what was to become the largest organization of any single racial group in American history, and which, as one of its supporters boasted to a German audience soon after the outbreak of the war, was to enjoy "the distinction of being the most widespread German body that the world has ever seen."[7] In 1914 it claimed a membership of two million. While its greatest strength lay in Pennsylvania, Wisconsin, New York, Ohio, Indiana, Illinois, and Iowa, it had well-organized branches in thirty-three other states of the Union. In Pennsylvania its membership rose to 100,000; in Wisconsin to 37,000; and in Illinois to 20,000. In the city of New York it claimed to have 24,000 members, in St. Louis, 20,000, and in some small German communities almost the entire adult population was affiliated with it.[8]

The Alliance was formed by a federation of existing German-American organizations. Locally these organizations were grouped into city Alliances (*Stadtverbände*) or branches (*Zweigverbände*). These in turn were federated into state Alliances (*Staatsverbände*), and the states collectively constituted the National Alliance (*Nationalbund*). Each branch set up committees to formulate its policy and to carry out its decisions, the most important generally being the legislative committee, which represented its interests before the various departments of local and state governments. A similar division of functions was characteristic of the national organization,

[7] Speech of Louis Viereck in the Hall of the Prussian Diet, Berlin. *The Fatherland* (New York), vol. 1, no. 15, p. 11 (November 8, 1914).

[8] According to a statement made by Hexamer in Chicago on December 8, 1915, the Alliance membership exceeded two and a half million. See *Mitteilungen des Deutschamerikanischen Nationalbundes der Vereinigten Staaten von Amerika; Bulletin of the National German-American Alliance* (Philadelphia, 1909–18), January, 1916, p. 6. Of the 280 inhabitants of the village of Gladstone, North Dakota, in February, 1915, 100 were found to be members of the Alliance. *Ibid.*, March, 1915, p. 24. See also the issues for October, 1914, p. 6, and September, 1915, pp. 3, 51; the pamphlet *Im Kampfe für Wahrheit und Recht* (German-American Literary Defense Committee, New York, 1915), 6; *New York Times*, July 23, 1916; *Germania-Herold* (Milwaukee), September 30, October 1, 1914; *Milwaukee-Sonntagspost*, July 23, 1916; and Michael Singer, *Jahrbuch der Deutschen in Chicago* (Singer, Chicago, 1916), 284.

which in 1914 also had two very able spokesmen in Congress in the persons of Richard Bartholdt of Missouri and Henry Vollmer of Iowa.[9]

The Alliance derived considerable help and strength from the German-language press. While publishing a monthly bulletin of its proceedings for circulation among its members, it claimed every German-American newspaper as its mouthpiece. Among its officials it numbered a long list of editors, whose columns were naturally favorable to its points of view.[10] Its activities were always front-page news, and long and sympathetic editorials often gave emphasis to its decisions. Wherever the German-American newspaper men were well organized, as they were in Wisconsin, for example, they were usually ready to follow its lead.[11]

Though only American citizens were eligible for membership, the many thousands of Germans whom it helped to obtain their papers were always a source of strength to the Alliance: "those are the recruits who are later to fight our battles."[12] An immigration committee was set up to look after those who had just arrived from the fatherland. In one circular after another, Germans resident in the United States were urged to become citizens. Under the title *Intro-*

[9] Bartholdt never held a prominent office in the Alliance, perhaps because of his preoccupation with congressional duties, but according to his close friend J. Otto Pfeiffer, editor of the *Westliche Post* (St. Louis), he was a member. Vollmer was president of the Central Verein of Scott and Davenport counties, Iowa. It was Bartholdt who secured a national charter for the Alliance in 1907.

[10] On the front page of every issue of its bulletin, *Mitteilungen,* appeared the statement: "Der Deutschamerikanische Nationalbund sieht in der gesamten deutschamerikanischen Presse sein Organ und ersucht dieselbe um grösstmögliche Verbreitung seiner Mitteilungen." Among the newspaper editors who held important positions in the Alliance were George Seibel of the *Volksblatt und Freiheits-Freund* (Pittsburgh); Max E. Socha of the *Germania* (Los Angeles); Jacob Schäfer of the *Washington Staatszeitung* (Seattle); Valentin J. Peter of the *Omaha Tribüne;* and Brand of the *Staats-Anzeiger* (Bismarck, North Dakota).

[11] The Verein der deutschen Presse von Wisconsin joined the Wisconsin Alliance in 1914. *Germania-Herold,* September 15, 1914.

[12] Adolph Timm, at a meeting of the legislative committee of the Central Alliance of Pennsylvania in November, 1914. *Mitteilungen,* December, 1914, p. 3.

duction to the Attainment of Citizenship, the Alliance issued
free of charge a manual for their instruction. German transla-
tions were also made of state constitutions and other public
documents; the Wisconsin Alliance, for example, distributed
at least five thousand of these to candidates for citizenship
between August, 1915, and July, 1916. The legislative committees of every branch were to be at the disposal of all such
candidates, and those who failed to obtain locally the help
they desired were invited to communicate with the central
organization in Philadelphia.[13]

After 1914 the Alliance extended its influence considerably
when other organizations began to cooperate. Among these
was the Roman Catholic Central Verein, which had hitherto
been somewhat hostile. In Montana and Oregon a working
agreement on certain questions was reached with the Socialist
Party.[14] In St. Louis new support came from "Free Thinkers,
Catholics, Protestants, Socialists, and all other elements of
German and Austrian extraction."[15] But the largest reinforce-
ments came from Irish sources. As early as January 25, 1907,
the Alliance had reached an agreement with the Ancient
Order of Hibernians "for the good of this Republic," whereby
both were to oppose entanglements of any kind "with any
foreign power"; to prevent the enactment of "laws abridging
the personal liberties of citizens"; and to combat the "restric-
tion of immigration of healthy persons from Europe."[16] By

[13] *Ibid.,* August, 1914, p. 9; September, 1914, p. 8; *Germania-Herold,* September 8, 1914; *Milwaukee-Sonntagspost,* July 23, 1916.

[14] *New-Yorker Staats-Zeitung,* May 9, 1916.

[15] *Mississippi Blätter* (St. Louis), February 28, 1915. Thus, frequently after
1914, the history of the Alliance merges with that of other organizations, and
it will often be impossible to treat it as a separate entity.

[16] *Boston Daily Globe,* January 25, 1907, quoted in *National German-American Alliance: Hearings before the Subcommittee of the Committee on the
Judiciary, United States Senate, 65 Congress, 2 Session, on S. 3529,* a bill to
repeal "An Act to Incorporate the National German-American Alliance,"
approved February 25, 1907 (hereafter cited as *Hearings on the German-
American Alliance*), p. 645. The clause opposing entanglements was obviously
dictated by the Irish, who resented any entente with Great Britain, whereas the
clause regarding "personal liberties" was clearly in line with the anti-
prohibition activities of the Alliance.

RICHARD BARTHOLDT

German-American Congressman Who Secured a Charter for the National German-American Alliance in 1907

1914 other Irish organizations, such as the Clan-na-Gael and the American Truth Society, were willing to be included in the pact, and in some localities Irish-German Leagues and Boards of Mutual Conference were set up.

In 1914, therefore, the German position in the United States was one of considerable strength. Of all the foreign-born elements the German-Americans were by far the best organized. While their tradition in this country was one of sincere patriotic devotion from the days of the Revolution on, they had clung tenaciously to the cultural heritage of their European fatherland. In some localities the circulation of their daily press exceeded that in the English tongue. Many of them enjoyed the privilege of bringing up their children in the language of their fathers, even in American grade schools, and in some cities, notably Cincinnati, Cleveland, and Milwaukee, many non-German children (negro, indeed, as well as white, it has been alleged) were receiving their daily instruction in German.[17] In rural Wisconsin not a few native Americans grew up speaking German according to the dialect of their ancestors and English with an accent. Prominent officials of the Alliance, like Leo Stern of Milwaukee and Hermann J. Lensner of Cleveland, held positions as supervisors of schools, and in some universities the German departments were affiliated solidly with the organization.

Had this movement derived its inspiration from Berlin? Was the Alliance, as was charged, "the mouthpiece of Pan-

---

[17] In 1914 the German-language dailies had a combined circulation of approximately 620,000; the semi-weeklies, 37,000; and the weeklies, 1,753,000. The *New-Yorker Staats-Zeitung* had a circulation of 70,000; the *Illinois Staats-Zeitung* (Chicago), 47,500; the *Germania-Herold* (Milwaukee), 24,000; and *Germania* (Milwaukee), a weekly, 100,000. *American Newspaper Annual and Directory*, 1914 (Ayer, Philadelphia, 1914), 1253–1259).

Wisconsin had a law permitting the study of a foreign language in the grade schools if parents wanted their children to take it. The school board of Milwaukee so interpreted the rule as to require all children, from the first grade up, to take German unless parents took definite steps to exempt them. See *Hearings on the German-American Alliance*, 100–101. German might be taught in the grade schools of Nebraska, Minnesota, and Indiana if a sufficient number of parents desired it. See *ibid.*, 102. At a meeting of the city Alliance

German ideas in America,"[18] and had it "in very large measure done the work in the United States of the Pan-German Union"?[19] As we examine the evidence today, it becomes increasingly clear that, not only was the Alliance reluctant to follow a German lead, but it was at times considerably at variance with it. The fact that the Pan-German Union of Germany maintained in the United States a separate organization, also known as the Pan-German Union, would seem to indicate that it hardly regarded the Alliance as the instrument of its policy.[20] Nor could the Alliance have favored Pan-German ideas when it refused, in October, 1908, to join the German Flottenverein.[21] A Pan-German movement, working for the aggrandizement of German interests throughout the world, would surely have welcomed the affiliation of the many German societies in Canada, yet the Alliance not only refused this affiliation but declared itself unwilling, in August, 1915, to intercede with the American government on behalf of the Germans in Canada, on the grounds that it was concerned, on this continent, only with the welfare of persons who were citizens of the United States.[22] It is also doubtful whether a Pan-German movement would have allowed non-Germans to hold high office, as did Professor Marion Dexter Learned of the University of Pennsylvania, who was for many years on the executive committee of the National Alliance, and Professor Herbert F. Sanborn, president of the Tennessee

on April 3, 1915, it was reported that of the 5,000 children learning German in the grade schools of Cleveland, 2,300 came from families that were not German-speaking. See the *Volksblatt und Freiheits-Freund* (Pittsburgh), April 4, 1915. The charge that negro children in Cincinnati were taking instruction in German was made by President W. M. B. Faunce of Brown University, who visited the city in February, 1916. *Mitteilungen,* April, 1916, p. 23.

[18] Gustavus Ohlinger, *The German Conspiracy in American Education* (Doran, New York, 1919), 47.

[19] A witness, in *Hearings on the German-American Alliance*, 95.

[20] This was the Alldeutscher Verband, some of the activities of which are reported in the *New-Yorker Staats-Zeitung,* August 4, 1914. It was never able to gain a very large following in the United States.

[21] *Hearings on the German-American Alliance,* 349.

[22] *New-Yorker Staats-Zeitung,* July 28, 1915; *Mitteilungen,* September, 1915, p. 59.

Alliance. Neither of these men could boast of German descent, but they had been invited to assume prominent positions in the organization as teachers of the German language and as interpreters of German culture.[23]

When the New York lawyer Theodore Sutro, who had been president of the New York State Alliance and editor of the Hearst-owned *Deutsches Journal,* went to Germany on a lecture tour between October, 1913, and February, 1914, he was surprised at the general ignorance of what the Germans had accomplished in the United States. "Instead of any influence or direction from German Imperial sources," he said, "I found that German statesmen and public men were eager to learn what the aims and objects of the National German-American Alliance really were. I found that this great Alliance was practically unknown to the German Government and German people, and that they rather looked upon it askance and with suspicion, until I explained that its chief aim was to preserve the German language and literature, besides the English, and all the other cultural ideals which it had written in its Constitution and By-Laws and in its Charter."[24]

At the eighth annual convention of the Alliance, on August 2, 1915, Hexamer lamented the absence, in German official circles, of "a sympathetic understanding of the nature of the German-American Alliance." In an article reprinted from the Philadelphia *Sonntags-Gazette,* the Alliance bulletin for September, 1915, regretted that there were always too many representatives of the German Empire in consular positions who, with the characteristic lack of enlightenment of German bureaucracy, were easily inclined to misjudge the German-Americans and their press. And Ambassador Bernstorff has

[23] Learned represented the Alliance at Leipzig in August, 1914, at the Kongress deutscher Geisteskultur und Deutschtum im Auslande. *Mitteilungen,* August, 1914, p. 8. See also *Viereck's American Weekly* (New York), vol. 6, no. 13 (May 2, 1917), 213.
[24] *Hearings on the German-American Alliance,* 141.

frankly admitted that "the question of the German-Americans has never been dealt with tactfully in Germany."[25]

The conclusion therefore seems inevitable that the German-American Alliance did not owe its rise to power to any guidance from Germany, but that it must have been the product of peculiarly American conditions. And these are not hard to discern. For it is in the prohibition question that we find the whole clue to German-American solidarity. Prohibition, always the abomination of the German-Americans, became an imminent issue after 1900. By them it was regarded as an attack upon age-long traditions and social customs and as an infringement of individual rights. "We must bear in mind," wrote the president of Hamilton City Alliance, of Ohio, in January, 1915, "that the efforts of the fanatics are directed primarily against us Germans. German manners and customs, and the joviality of the German people, are a thorn in the flesh of these gentlemen."[26] Thus, as the prohibition movement went forward in the United States, the German-American Alliance rose to power as a defensive organization—a *Schutz- und Trutz-Bund,* as its secretary called it in 1903.[27] Had prohibition not become a burning issue in local and national politics, we might even doubt whether the German-American Alliance would ever have been heard of outside a few German-speaking groups of a purely academic nature.

The Alliance was what it was in 1914 by virtue of a hard struggle against the Anti-Saloon League and other prohibitionist organizations. In its inception essentially a cultural movement, it had encountered in prohibition the greatest menace to the Germans—not of Germany but of the United States — and had therefore given the best of its efforts to a

---

[25] *Mitteilungen,* September, 1915, pp. 2, 50; Johann H. von Bernstorff, *My Three Years in America* (Skeffington, London, 1920), 19.
[26] *Mitteilungen,* February, 1915, p. 4.
[27] *German-American Annals,* 1:54 (1903).

fight against it.[28] "The Alliance," its press bureau at Philadelphia announced on August 1, 1915, "has, since the beginning, made it its task to overthrow the false teachings of the
fanatics of prohibition, and has neglected no opportunity of
helping the citizens of the United States to retain their
personal liberty."[29] At the same time, in an article in its
monthly organ entitled "Why the National Alliance Fights
Unceasingly against Prohibition," it was declared:

Prohibition signifies the annihilation of the principle for which
the War of Independence was waged and carried through vic-
toriously. It means that thought, speech, and action shall be laid
in fetters. It means that the misdemeanors of a few individuals
shall be avenged upon the whole American nation.

In order to gain for the Germans of America that place in the
sun which has hitherto always been denied them, it is absolutely
necessary that they enjoy personal liberty, and that this shall not
be whittled away by the attacks of the prohibitionists and the
persecutors of the foreign-born.[30]

In every district where prohibition threatened, state and
city Alliances set up a Committee for Personal Freedom to
carry on the fight, and the legislative committees watched
over the legislatures. The press bureau of the National
Alliance kept a careful eye upon every state, in every election,
and noted each public demonstration and expression of
opinion, both for and against prohibition. Before each election lists of candidates for Congress, state legislatures, and
local public offices were drawn up, and notes were made
upon the eligibility of each from the standpoint of the wet-
or-dry issue. Just as many an aspirant for political honors
dropped from public life for having incurred the enmity of
the Anti-Saloon League, so not a few managed to achieve

---

[28] According to Mr. Siegmund G. von Bosse, the Alliance favored the fight
against prohibition in order to gain German-American support for its cultural
program. Statement to the writer, Philadelphia, October 6, 1937.
[29] *Milwaukee-Sonntagspost*, August 1, 1915.
[30] *Mitteilungen*, August, 1915, p. 4.

success because the Alliance gave them its support. Indeed it is hard to find any other important issue in German-American affairs before 1914, for the reports of the state Alliances in the monthly bulletin are devoted almost exclusively to this question.[31]

In 1900 the Prohibition Party inaugurated an unusually militant campaign, and also declared itself in favor of female suffrage. Between 1904 and 1906 more prohibition candidates were elected to state legislatures than ever before. In July, 1908, the party threw down what was taken as a challenge by the German element, when at its national convention at Columbus it adopted in its platform a plank demanding "legislation basing suffrage only upon intelligence and ability to read and write the English language." The Anti-Saloon League, an organization even more virile and realistic in its methods than the Prohibition Party, began to find local politicians more and more inclined to listen to its demands, especially when the club of a hostile vote was swung menacingly about their heads. County option, and then state prohibition, became realities. In 1907 Georgia went dry, being the first state to do so since 1899, and between July, 1907, and January, 1909, she was followed by five other southern states.[32]

It was apparent that the country was taking prohibition seriously. The German-Americans, who for many years had enjoyed their local *Turnvereine, Liederkränze, Männerchöre,* and other clubs, naturally began to see in federation the surest means of defense. Thus Alliances sprang into being, and the more effective their stand against prohibition the more powerful they became. As early as September, 1903, the

---

[31] Seven of the sixteen pages of *Mitteilungen* for August, 1914, deal entirely with prohibition. In the September issue, the first after the outbreak of war in Europe, the reports from Washington, North Dakota, Michigan, and Texas mention little else.

[32] Leigh Colvin, *Prohibition in the United States: A History of the Prohibition Party and of the Prohibition Movement* (Doran, New York, 1926), 306 ff., 338.

National Alliance, at its second convention at Baltimore, drew up resolutions against the "blue laws" and against the type of temperance propaganda that was slowly being injected into the schoolbooks. In 1904 it sent its president, Hexamer, to appear before the House Committee of the Judiciary in firm opposition to the Hepburn-Dolliver Bill.[33]

Prohibition was the sole *raison d'être* of many of the local Alliances before the war. The formation of the Brooklyn Alliance, subsequently one of the strongest branches in the country, was a typical example. In July, 1907, when the National Alliance was mentioned at a meeting of the Brooklyn Turnverein, "it came to light that only a little was known about the existence of this Alliance." A committee was appointed to study its aims, with a view to affiliation. Delegates were sent to the fourth convention of the Alliance in New York, between October 4 and October 7, 1907, but there seemed little eagerness to form a branch in Brooklyn. Then, unexpectedly, "there fell, like a bombshell," the decision of the New York Supreme Court judge, O'Gorman, that the old Sunday laws in the state charter were still valid and were to be enforced. This stimulated the Germans of Brooklyn to action, and the result was the formation of an Alliance on December 27, which by June of the following year had a membership of twelve thousand. Similarly, the Alliance of Jackson came into being early in 1908, and was soon followed by the formation of a state Alliance, when the Anti-Saloon League began its "agitation against personal liberty in the state of Michigan." "We can now proceed in unity against the rantings of the nativists and the enemies of individual freedom," it was proclaimed after this Alliance had been formed. The Alliances of Missouri and Illinois had

[33] Albert B. Faust, *The German Element in the United States* (new ed., Steuben Society, New York, 1927), 2:147–149. The bill aimed to prohibit the importation of alcoholic liquors from other states by persons resident in "dry" states. The Alliance persuaded the House Committee to amend it so as to permit such importation if the alcoholic liquors were for private use.

admitted in 1905 that it was as a result of a campaign against
Sunday licensing that "our Alliance became widely known
throughout the whole area, and thereby steadily won more
supporters in St. Louis, as well as in other cities like Kansas
City, St. Joseph, Joplin, Sedalia, etc." Likewise in Ohio a
special drive against prohibition, initiated in March, 1906,
and led by Simon Hickler of the Cleveland *Wächter und
Anzeiger,* was regarded as having "helped the Alliance to a
position of power" in the state.[34]

By 1914 the Alliance was being handsomely subsidized—not
by the German government, however, but by the American
brewers. In the early summer of 1913 one Percy Andreae, the
self-styled president of a brewers' and liquor dealers' organization called the National Association of Commerce and
Labor, offered to supply the Alliance with funds for an
intensive campaign against prohibition. Andreae had been
working with the president of the Ohio Alliance, through
whom he came into contact with officers of the national
organization. The outcome was an agreement with Joseph
Keller, a vice-president of the National Alliance, and
Hexamer, which was concluded in Philadelphia. The National Association of Commerce and Labor was to do its
work behind the mask of the Alliance, paying money over to
John Tjarks, its treasurer. This money was to be held as a
separate propaganda fund. In the first year the Alliance drew
twelve thousand dollars under this agreement, which sum was
expended to send out speakers and to distribute literature. A
Committee for Organization and Publication, under Keller's
supervision, was also set up.[35]

With Andreae's financial backing the Alliance was able to
widen its field of activity considerably. In December, 1913,

[34] Heinrici, *Das Buch der Deutschen,* 833–834, 836, 849–857, 862–863.
[35] *Hearings on the German-American Alliance,* 205–206, 207–209, 213–214,
216, 220–221, 231–232, 282; *Brewing and Liquor Interests and German Propaganda: Hearings before a Subcommittee of the Committee on the Judiciary*
(United States Senate, 65 Congress, 2 Session, September, 1918), 840.

when the Hobson, Sheppard, and Works resolutions were
before Congress, its agents became active in Washington.
Hexamer, who was in the capital, promised to have four
million protests entered against these measures. On December
29, after returning to Philadelphia, he reported to Andreae
that he had appointed "a number of prominent residents,
who are members of our District of Columbia branch, to form
a standing legislative committee of the National German-
American Alliance in Washington." The chairman of this
committee was the Honorable Simon Wolf, "who is—which
is very important for our purpose—one of, if not the most
influential of Jews in the United States," and who would
therefore "bring in a vigorous and persistent element of our
population to work for us." This committee, to which
Hexamer referred in a subsequent letter as "our lobbying
committee," was to be maintained at the expense of Andreae
and the brewers.[36]

On March 14, 1914, Hexamer reported with some satisfaction that "our committee in Washington is working ex-
cellently and in the right direction." Keller's Committee for
Organization and Publication also made a promising start.
An intensive campaign was carried on in Texas in 1914, in
Illinois and Ohio in 1915, and in Missouri and Indiana in
1916.[37] In November, 1914, the bulletin of the Alliance,
hardly anticipating the unhappy day when a congressional
investigation would throw more light upon the matter, honored Keller with a front-page portrait as "an orator who has
come forth against prohibition and for personal freedom, and
who, in numerous appeals and circulars, has aroused the
German-American voters to play an impressive part in the
election campaign."[38]

Meanwhile, Henry Thuenen, secretary of the Iowa Brew-

---

[36] *Hearings on the German-American Alliance*, 222, 227–228, 229; *Brewing
and Liquor Interests*, 900.
[37] *Hearings on the German-American Alliance*, 287–289.
[38] *Mitteilungen*, November, 1914, p. 1.

ers' Association, had, on January 27, 1914, discovered it to be "high time for a start to be made with the German-American Alliance in this state."[39] By May, 1914, he and the Iowa Alliance were working together against local prohibition. The correspondence between Keller and his chief propagandist, Robert L. Soergel, describes the growth of many new branches, and rather suggests that the arrangement was more beneficial to the Alliance than to the brewers.[40] This was apparently above all true of Texas, where the chief interest was shown by German pastors and college professors and where the "beer goat could not be ridden too hard, but the idealistic aims of the Alliance chiefly emphasized."[41] In parts of Illinois, Soergel found that "the German-speaking citizens were in many instances total strangers to each other," but by March 26, 1915, he was able cheerfully to report that "our organization has made an inroad."[42]

The Alliance had begun to mobilize its heaviest forces in a drive against national prohibition when war broke out in Europe. Whatever change of policy this new crisis might necessitate, and however diverting might be the need to rally to the cause of the fatherland, the German-Americans were urged again and again not to lose sight of their own fight against prohibition. H. C. Bloedel of the Allegheny County Alliance of Pennsylvania, at an executive committee meeting of October 25, 1914, expressed the duty of the German-Americans. "In these very serious days of grave events in the old Fatherland," he said, "we must not become blind to the earnest problems to be solved in our country of adoption. It is our chief duty to serve this country first. While the news from the battlefields, and the supreme achievements of our

---

[39] *Hearings on the German-American Alliance*, 243, 245.
[40] This correspondence is published in *Brewing and Liquor Interests*, 1279 ff.
[41] *Ibid.*, 1285.
[42] *Ibid.*, 873. On February 13, 1915, another organization, the Liquor Dealers' Protective League, made overtures to the New Jersey Alliance, in a letter to its president, E. C. Stahl. The latter, however, pointed out in reply that the New Jersey Alliance would feel itself more effective in the fight against prohibition if it retained its independence. *Mitteilungen*, May, 1915, p. 19.

kin abroad, of which we daily receive report, make our hearts rejoice, we must always keep in mind the great struggle before us in the election of November 3. The law of self-preservation demands that we redouble our energies toward the attainment of our objectives."[43]

The unanimous German response to the call to arms in Europe was repeatedly held up as an inspiration to the German-Americans in their activities over here. Yet war and prohibition, urged Judge John Schwaab, president of the Ohio Alliance, at its annual convention at Canton on August 21, 1915, should be treated, so far as possible, as "separate issues." Bearing in mind that many opponents of prohibition were also opponents of Germany, those who addressed non-German audiences on domestic topics should always sedulously soft-pedal the war question. "Let us drive no friend out of our camp by making the European war our war." Hence mass meetings continued to be held, as at Richmond, Virginia, on September 20, 1914, at which speakers gave all their attention to prohibition and none to the war.[44]

The extent to which the Alliance participated in the elections of 1914 showed that no international problems could divert it completely from the fight against prohibition. Andreae himself went among many of its branches to campaign for "wet" candidates. On August 1 the Ohio Alliance, always deeply immersed in local politics, presented the secretary of state at Columbus with 280,000 signatures against prohibition. Meeting in convention at Toledo from August 21 to 23, it declared itself prepared to answer the challenge of the Anti-Saloon League, as also that of the equally obnoxious advocates of female suffrage, "through whom the fanatics of prohibition are planning to gain everything else that remains to be desired by them in the state." The Alliance of St. Louis pledged its members to vote for no candidate

[43] Hearings on the German-American Alliance, 313.
[44] Cincinnatier Freie Presse, August 22, 1915; Mitteilungen, September, 1915, p. 46; Milwaukee-Sonntagspost, September 20, 1914.

whose name was not on its list of eligibles. In Michigan, where a petition of 117,000 signatures had been drawn up against prohibition, the Alliance boasted the defeat of a bill to put clubs and a number of drinking fraternities under rigid state supervision. The Wisconsin Alliance, at its annual convention, spent much of its time deciding which candidates were worthy of German-American support, and published a list of its favorites on August 25. From Pennsylvania there came news of a so-called Personal Liberty Party, which the Alliance was prepared to support in several local contests. When, in the Texas primaries, the "dry" candidates were all defeated, the Alliance claimed most of the credit. The Indiana Alliance sent to Washington a hundred thousand signatures against prohibition, to which the Nebraska Alliance added another forty thousand. In Kentucky the state Alliance devoted itself almost exclusively to prohibition at its annual convention on September 6 and 7, preparing to rally the German-American vote, in the next two months, behind its chosen candidates for the Senate and the governorship.[45]

An interest equally keen was manifested by the national organization. Through Andreae it was provided with the names of suitable candidates for public office in a dozen states. On August 29 it published in the German-language press an appeal to the German-Americans to elect only "liberal minded" representatives to their state legislatures and to Congress.[46] In September its press bureau threatened a large-scale political offensive against the Anti-Saloon League and its

[45] *Volksblatt und Freiheits-Freund*, October 25, December 6, 1914; *New-Yorker Staats-Zeitung*, August 3, 1914; *Cincinnatier Freie Presse*, August 2, September 8, 1914; *Germania-Herold*, September 8, 19, 1914; *Westliche Post*, October 15, 1914; *Milwaukee-Sonntagspost*, November 15, 1914; *Germania* (Milwaukee), August 25, 1914. For an account of the political methods employed by the Wisconsin Alliance, see *Hearings on the German-American Alliance*, 122. With reference to candidates in local elections the Central Alliance of Pennsylvania boasted, "Sie wissen, dass es politischer Selbstmord ist, wenn sie für Local Option stimmen." *Mitteilungen*, June, 1915, p. 19.

[46] The appeal was signed by Hexamer and Timm. *New-Yorker Staats-Zeitung*, August 29, 1914; *Hearings on the German-American Alliance*, 241–242.

allies: "hereby we suggest the lines of future activity for the German element, which has every reason to engage itself in politics." On October 2 another appeal from the National Alliance enjoined the German-American voters to forget party loyalty if the candidate of their affiliation was in favor of prohibition. In a last-minute circular, at the end of the month, the election was described as "no mere drink question." "In this election campaign," it was added with an unmistakable touch of hyperbole, "it is as much a matter of 'to be or not to be' for the racial heritage of the German-Americans, as it is over there for the Germans and Austro-Hungarians on the battlefields of Belgium, France, and Russia."[47]

After the outbreak of war it became a common trick of Alliance orators to treat prohibition as a British importation. Thus *Mitteilungen* of September, 1914, inveighed against "the intolerance, the hypocrisy, the hatred of the German, and the Puritanism that have been implanted here by the English." "Over there," ran a report drawn up by John Schwaab of the Ohio Alliance in July, 1915, "it is the annihilation of the German nation on account of its commercial growth; over here, it is the suppression of the Germanic influence, which is a thorn in the flesh of the Englishman. The drink question is forced upon us by the same hypocritical Puritans as over there are endeavoring to exterminate the German nation." "The National Alliance," added Hans Demuth of South Dakota, a newly elected vice-president, at the close of the eighth convention in August, 1915, "leads the struggle against Anglo-Saxonism, against the fanatical enslavers of political and personal liberty; it fights sinister Knownothingism, British influence, and the zealotism and the servile Puritanism that have come over from England."[48]

[47] *Milwaukee-Sonntagspost*, September 20, November 1, 1914; *Volksblatt und Freiheits-Freund*, October 3, 1914; *Mitteilungen*, November, 1914, p. 6.
[48] *Mitteilungen*, September, 1914, p. 4; August, 1915, p. 19; September, 1915, p. 4.

A study of the German-American Alliance in the three years of American neutrality thus begins with the question of prohibition rather than with the foreign politics of the German Empire. It is in the proceedings of the various state legislatures, and not in the *Alldeutsche Blätter* of the Pan-German Union, that one finds the most pertinent records of its early history. The German-American leaders obtained their training in public affairs not from Berlin but from American politics. Their organization, the Alliance, however persistently it might profess, and even pursue, a German cultural purpose, was essentially the product of American social and political conditions, and its violently pro-German attitude after 1914 should not be allowed to delude us into reading its history backwards, and make us lose sight of its truly American origin. While very much alive to domestic politics before the war, it manifested surprisingly little interest in foreign relations. In its organization it followed the democratic prototype of all other American institutions, formulating its policy not according to imperial decree, but through resolutions put to the vote of its members.

Hence to talk about Pan-Germanism as existing on a large scale in this country, and to conceive of the German-Americans, in the words of William Roscoe Thayer, as "most ready to bow down and do homage to a Hohenzollern as their accepted overlord" was either to display an amazing ignorance of native conditions or deliberately to distort the facts for some ulterior purpose. Even to represent the Alliance as endeavoring to make itself the instrument of German policy before 1914 was to shut one's eyes to the many and all-absorbing problems with which its members were faced in the necessity of adjusting themselves to the social conditions of the New World.[49]

[49] Thayer, *Life and Letters of Hay*, 2:290. According to Thayer, it was the German ambassador, von Holleben, who fed the kaiser with stories of German-American loyalty to the Empire, but this would not seem to be substantiated by the correspondence of von Holleben in *Die Grosse Politik*. Not one of the

The whole theme of German-American history in these years is inevitably one of adjustment to American life and of reaction to American social forces, such as prohibition, which to a foreign-born element was something not only alien but incomprehensible. Thus that history is apt to be one of conflict—not conflict with established authority as such (for who has more respect for authority, law, and public discipline than the German?), but conflict with the older, often consciously anti-alien element in American life. The outbreak of war in Europe only accentuated the conflict, when the German-Americans naturally displayed an unreserved sympathy with the land of their birth (a land which they knew from their own youth, but which its enemies were misrepresenting before the eyes of the ignorant), and when the older element seemed often just as inclined to join hands with the other side.

It was not long before the whole question became crystallized in the attitude of the Alliance toward Wilson. More and more it came to identify the president with the hostile element in American public life: even in 1914 his British ancestry was repeatedly cited as grounds for suspicion. As the war progressed, and the neutrality of America began to work to the detriment of the Central Powers, the animosity of the Alliance became more and more pronounced. Thus the general conflict which we have mentioned resolved itself into a more specific antagonism between that organization and the administration, culminating in attempts to destroy Wilson politically in 1916. It is with this antagonism as its central theme that the following study of the Alliance in the three years of American neutrality will be made.

highly confidential documents of the Alliance published by the two Senate inquiries of 1918 and 1919 (see notes 16 and 35 above) revealed the slightest suspicion of any direct connection between the Alliance and the German government.

I I

"DER DEUTSCHE MICHEL
IST AUFGEWACHT!"[1]

THE EXCITEMENT AROUSED IN THE UNITED STATES AS A WHOLE
by the European war was experienced with intensity by the
German-American Alliance. For August, 1914, it had anticipated nothing more absorbing than the unveiling of a
monument to Von Steuben at Utica, New York. Ambassador
von Bernstorff was to have been the principal speaker, and
the ceremony was to have been followed by three days of
pageantry illustrative of the history of the Mohawk Valley.
With the intervention of the European crisis, Bernstorff was
called away to more trying tasks. His toga fell upon Professor
Hugo Münsterberg of Harvard, who took advantage of the
occasion to represent Von Steuben as the "symbol of war's
romanticism and idealism" and as "the first German exchange
professor in the soldier's coat," whose monument would
"stand as an appeal to the world never to forget the ties which
bind the United States and Germany." Following Münsterberg's speech the gathering drew up resolutions expressing resentment at the general misrepresentation of the
German cause in the United States and hopes for an early
German victory.[2]

To have lived in New York or Chicago in that boisterous
first week of August, 1914, or in any other large American
city where a considerable portion of the population had been
drawn immediately from the nations then at war, was to have
lived vicariously the excitement of nearly every European

[1] Headlines in the *New-Yorker Staats-Zeitung*, August 7, 1914.
[2] *Mitteilungen*, September, 1914, p. 3; *Milwaukee Free Press*, August 2,
1914; *New York Times*, August 4, 1914; *Cincinnatier Freie Presse*, August 7,
1914.

capital. German-language newspapers issued calls to the colors to all German reservists, and the German consuls were faced, for a time, with almost as big a problem of organization as the German general staff. *Deutschland über Alles* resounded as lustily from the processions along Broadway as in Unter den Linden. According to one observer, Hoboken might have been a suburb of Berlin. To the editor of the *Cincinnatier Freie Presse* it was a reminder of "the glorious days of '70." Irish nationalists joined hands with Russian Jews in wishing success to the Central Powers. Chicago had a little European war of its own, when Teuton and Slav, each demonstrating violently his sympathy for the cause of his native country, came into open conflict. On Sunday, August 2, thousands of New York German-Americans marched, despite the terrific heat, to the Bavarian *Volksfest* in Harlem River Park and, amidst robust and prolonged cheers, sent off a telegram of greeting and good wishes to King Ludwig. Branches of the Alliance frequently furnished the reservists with hospitality as they passed through their various localities. In New York the United German Societies opened a fund for them, and in St. Louis the city Alliance set out to find employment for those whose return to Germany became more and more unlikely.[3]

On August 2 the Commercial Cable Company gave notice that all cables to England must henceforth be in English and subject to censorship.[4] This was but premonitory of the effect that the war was to have upon the communication of news between the United States and Europe. Very soon afterward, when Great Britain entered the war, amidst a howl of execration from the German-language papers, the German trans-

[3] *New-Yorker Staats-Zeitung*, August 3, 4, 1914; *Cincinnatier Freie Presse*, August 5, 6, 1914; *Illinois Staats-Zeitung* (Chicago), July 30, 1914; *Westliche Post* (St. Louis), August 29, 1914. The text of the message to King Ludwig is given in the *New-Yorker Staats-Zeitung*, August 3, 1914. According to the *Cincinnatier Freie Presse* of August 5, 1914, the Russian Jews of Cincinnati were planning the formation of a regiment of volunteers to embark with the German reservists in the service of the Central Powers.
[4] *New-Yorker Staats-Zeitung*, August 3, 1914.

Atlantic cable was severed, and henceforth Germany found herself at a disadvantage in presenting her version of the news in this country.

Equally disconcerting was the tendency on the part of many American journalists to point to Germany as the aggressor. Editorial comment upon the war was often far from impartial. Frank Cobb of the New York *World* argued on August 4 that "in the very vanguard of the twentieth century in most respects, Germany has struggled back to the seventeenth century politically." When on the following day his paper announced, "Germany has run amuck. . . . If the forces that the Kaiser has loosed are victorious, the map of European republicanism may as well be rolled up, and the American people prepare to make the last great stand for democracy," it was only saying a little more tersely what hundreds of newspapers were suggesting throughout the country.[5]

Here was a situation to which the German-Americans must give their immediate attention. At a meeting arranged by the Central Verein of Newark, New Jersey, on August 16, Hexamer declared that, as a born American, he had never felt greater cause to be ashamed of his country: "anything so mean, depraved, and mendacious as the Anglophile press of America would be impossible in any other civilized country."[6] If a stranger visiting the United States for the first time

---

[5] *World* (New York), August 4, 5, 1914. Cobb's editorial was entitled "Autocracy or Democracy." See also John L. Heaton, *Cobb of "The World"* (Dutton, New York, 1924), 251.

By mid-August the *Outlook*, the *Independent*, and *Harper's Weekly* had charged Germany with beginning the war, and editorials condemning Germany had appeared in the *North American* (Philadelphia), the *Springfield Republican*, the New York *Globe, Tribune, Times, Evening Post*, and *World*, the St. *Louis Republic*, the *Baltimore News*, and the *Salt Lake City Herald-Republican*. See the *Literary Digest*, 49:293–295 (August 22, 1914). Toward the end of 1914 the *Literary Digest* published the results of a questionnaire sent to 367 American editors, asking with which side their sympathies lay. In reply 105 stated that they favored the Allies; 20 the Central Powers; and 242 that they were neutral. See the issue for November 14, 1914, p. 939. See also James D. Squires, *British Propaganda at Home and in the United States from 1914 to 1917* (Harvard Historical Monographs, no. 6, Cambridge, 1935), 43–44.

[6] *New-Yorker Staats-Zeitung*, August 17, 1914; *Cincinnatier Freie Presse*, August 19, 1914.

should read some of the Anglo-American newspapers of those weeks, he later observed at Philadelphia, "he would come to the conclusion that the American nation should burn its Declaration of Independence, tear up its Constitution, and declare its people good and loyal subjects of King George." On August 3 he had outlined a program of counter-attack in an appeal which was printed with enthusiastic comment in most of the German-language newspapers. The National Alliance, he declared, was ready "to defend the German name against the hate and ignorance of a minority in this country." In every locality its branches should set up a "literary bureau," under the direction of a capable press agent, to controvert false information given in the Anglo-American newspapers. Collections were also to be organized for German war relief purposes.[7]

Mass protests from the German-Americans were their reply to unfriendly articles in the daily press. As early as July 31 the United German Societies of New York had demonstrated against the anti-German attitude of the metropolitan newspapers. "Mit Herz und Hand für's Vaterland" was the watchword of a mass meeting held in Chicago on August 4, which passed resolutions deploring the spread of racial prejudice in the United States. The next day three hundred German reservists marched through the city in a demonstration held by the Chicago Alliance, which was characterized by the *New-Yorker Staats-Zeitung* as a "patriotische Demonstration." As a result of these activities certain Chicago newspapers were said to have been scared away from the Allied cause. In Brooklyn, on August 7, Henry Weismann, president of the New York State Alliance, proclaimed a ban on the New York *World, Sun, Herald,* and *Telegraph.* "All that we ask for is fair play," resolved the Alliance of Cincinnati. In Boston the

---

[7] *Mitteilungen,* September, 1914, p. 1; November, 1914, pp. 21, 22; *New-Yorker Staats-Zeitung,* August 4, 1914; *Illinois Staats-Zeitung,* August 4, 1914; *Westliche Post,* August 6, 1914; *Volksblatt und Freiheits-Freund* (Pittsburgh), August 4, 1914.

Alliance arranged a mass meeting in Faneuil Hall, at which it allowed Socialist Deputy Freiman, of the Reichstag, to state the case for Germany.[8]

In Wisconsin the anti-Ally lead was taken by Leo Stern, president of the state Alliance, who, according to Francis Hackett, "believed in the idealism of Germany as a Catholic believes in the Immaculate Conception." At the German Day rally at Kenosha, on August 9, while disclaiming any intention of setting up "a 'Little Germany' in this country," he expressed the conviction that Germany would win, for where there was "truth, culture, civilization, and morality, there was also victory."[9] On August 28 he organized what was adjudged to be "the grandest and most impressive demonstration that Milwaukee has witnessed since the Civil War." Its resolutions, printed in large type on the front page of the *Free Press,* well illustrate the attitude of the Alliance toward the war:

We sympathize deeply with every English wife, whose husband has obeyed the call to arms; with every French mother, who is forced to yield her son . . .

We are fully convinced that all who have followed the course of events know that the dragon seed scattered by Russia in the Balkans ripened into a bloody harvest, which produced the Pan-Servian propaganda, culminating in the vile murder at Sarajevo, and that England, jealous of Germany's wonderful progress, and the deep-rooted feeling of revenge in France, will for all times be emblazoned on the pages of history as the real cause of this frightful catastrophe . . .

[8] *New-Yorker Staats-Zeitung,* August 1, 7, 8, 1914; *Illinois Staats-Zeitung,* August 5, 6, 1914; Singer's *Jahrbuch,* 1915, p. 14; *Germania* (Milwaukee), August 14, 1914; *Cincinnatier Freie Presse,* August 8, 1914; *Mitteilungen,* October, 1914, p. 16. According to *Germania* (August 14), the Chicago *Evening Post, Daily News, Herald,* and *Tribune* all became more friendly toward the German cause as a result of the demonstrations. By September 6, 1914, the *Sunday Tribune* was offering to its German-American readers a large picture of William II "hübsch in vier Farben gedrückt." Advertisement in the *Germania-Herold* (Milwaukee), September 5, 1914.

[9] Francis Hackett, "How Milwaukee Takes the War," in the *New Republic,* 3:272–273 (July 17, 1915); *Milwaukee Free Press,* August 10, 1914. Hackett interviewed Stern in collecting material for his article.

We appeal to the honor of the American press, and demand that it throw off the yoke which the English monopolized news service has placed upon it. . . .[10]

It has been said, with some sagacity, that the battle of Waterloo was won on the playing fields of Eton. Perhaps some historian will in future demonstrate, with equal conviction, that the World War was won in the newspaper columns of America. For it is now apparent that the literary campaign in the United States was ultimately as important as any particular piece of military strategy. Hence, realizing the significance of a stout "literary defense," the Alliance responded readily to Hexamer's appeal to set up organizations to watch the daily press. In Wisconsin a committee of five began to enlighten public opinion upon the German cause. At St. Louis a similar committee of seven turned its attention not only to the press but also to cinemas which displayed anti-German films. These cinemas were warned to choose programs of a different nature, or "be prepared for a boycott from the German element in the city."[11]

Most vigorous, however, were the measures taken in New York, for it was here that the "Press Cossacks," as the Milwaukee *Germania-Herold* called them, showed the strongest antipathy toward Germany. On August 19 an organization called the German-American Literary Defense Committee made its appearance with a manifesto in the *New-Yorker Staats-Zeitung* and other important German-language dailies. The individual, it was declared, could do little as such against the enormous power of the Anglo-American newspapers, "but united even the weak are strong." The committee therefore urged the German-Americans first of all to send their letters of protest to its office. Here they would be submitted to a sort

[10] *Milwaukee Free Press*, August 28, 29, 1914; *Mitteilungen*, October, 1914, p. 19. At this meeting the audience even cheered one speaker who praised the Belgians for the defense of their country.
[11] *Milwaukee Free Press*, August 19, 1914; *Westliche Post*, October 15, November 12, 1914.

of voluntary censorship, to insure that they were "free from provocation" and in no way injurious to the "carefully planned campaign of the committee." Those who were not accustomed to the use of the English language could submit their protests and petitions in German and have them translated by the committee.[12]

From this rather humble beginning there grew up the most influential of all the German-American propaganda centers. By the beginning of September the Literary Defense Committee was a flourishing organization, with Henry Weismann of the New York State Alliance as its leader. From its offices at 150 Nassau Street it began to send its publications to all parts of the country. Some of the pamphlets which it distributed, such as *The Truth about Germany,* compiled by the American Institute of Berlin, it imported from the fatherland, but the majority it issued itself. Among these were Houston Stewart Chamberlain's *Who Is to Blame for the War,* Professor William M. Sloane's *Fair Play and Neutrality,* and Professor John W. Burgess' *The Present Crisis in Europe.* Other writers who placed their talent at its disposal were Faust C. De Walsh, Dr. Hugo Schweitzer, Rudolf Cronau, and Thomas C. Hall.[13]

By the middle of November, 1914, the committee had distributed fifty-seven thousand pamphlets and found the demand for its literature still growing.[14] By the end of 1915 it reported that it had distributed a million pamphlets and leaflets, of which about half had been published at its own expense, adding that, as "the German and Austrian brain is not skilled in chicanery as is the English . . . we can only

[12] *Germania-Herold,* September 22, 1914; *New-Yorker Staats-Zeitung,* August 19, 1914; *Cincinnatier Freie Presse,* August 21, 1914.

[13] *New-Yorker Staats-Zeitung,* September 4, 1914; January 31, 1915; *Milwaukee-Sonntagspost,* October 25, 1914; *Im Kampfe für Wahrheit und Recht,* 12.

[14] "Man ist im Lande auf die deutsche Darstellung des Riesenkonflikts in Europa aufmerksam geworden. Sogar die Bücherei des Kongresses in Washington hat sich vom Ausschuss Material erbeten. Kirchen und Universitäten wenden sich an das Verteidigungs-Buro, um Klarheit zu erhalten." *Mitteilungen,* December, 1914, p. 8.

rely on truth to defend us, but we have found this a very
effective weapon." Everything up to that time, it claimed,
had been done on "the exceedingly small revenue of $6,000,"
all its labor being voluntary. In New York City much of its
literature had been distributed by German reservists. Its
funds had been raised mainly from contributions from members, who at the end of the war were to receive a "handsomely
engraved certificate" to show that "in this great world crisis
the recipient did his part in the liberation of this country
from British influences."[15]

At the beginning of 1915 there was talk of establishing a
daily newspaper in the English language. Hexamer had already expressed the satisfaction of the Alliance with Viereck's
English weekly, *The Fatherland,* and had frequently used it
as a means of conveying his messages to the non-German
public. On April 3, 1915, Weismann's name appeared as secretary of a Printers' and Publishers' Association, to which
subscriptions were invited in the German-language press.
The aim of the organization, it was stated, was to found a
new "fearless independent daily newspaper" in New York.
The response, however, proved disappointing, and the attempt was subsequently abandoned—possibly, to some extent, as a result of the secret acquisition by the German government of the New York *Mail and Express.*[16]

Other branches, less powerful than that of New York,
did their share to defend the German name. The Oklahoma
Alliance, through its secretary, Heinrich Schulz, instituted
an investigation of the editorial positions on American newspapers held by Englishmen. That a surprising number of
these positions were in English hands was, indeed, a common
insinuation of Alliance orators who would in this way ac-

[15] Mimeographed appeal issued by the committee in 1915, among the German-American pamphlets in the Library of Congress; *New-Yorker Staats-
Zeitung,* February 6, 1915.
[16] *Im Kampfe für Wahrheit und Recht,* 5; letter of Hexamer to the editor
of *The Fatherland,* vol. 1, no. 5, p. 2 (September 6, 1914). The project was
advertised in the *Cincinnatier Freie Presse,* April 3, 1915.

count for the anti-German tone of the American press. The Alliance of Washington, finding that the editor of the *Spokesman Review* was a British subject, demanded that the national organization work for a bill in Congress to require that all newspapers reveal the nationality of their editors and of the companies controlling them. In the early days of the war the bulletin of the Alliance declared large sections of the press to be under the "influence of the reptile funds of Downing Street," and continually denounced the anti-German newspapers as the tools of British financial interests.[17]

Propagandists from Germany received considerable cooperation from the various branches of the Alliance. The latter felt flattered to be able to arrange meetings for some of the distinguished speakers who were sent over. Thus Dr. Eugen Kühnemann, exchange professor from Breslau, spoke at large demonstrations organized by the Alliance in Pennsylvania, Indiana, and Washington. In Wisconsin, where he became, on June 26, 1915, an honorary member of the state Alliance, he was a great favorite, a box at one of his meetings selling for as much as $150. Another outstanding guest of the Wisconsin Alliance was the former German colonial minister, Dr. Bernhard Dernburg, who was invited to Milwaukee to address a large public gathering on December 11, 1914. There it was that he defended the German invasion of Belgium upon the supposedly American doctrine that "treaty obligations must not and cannot be kept if it is against policy to do so." While in Wisconsin he made, through Leo Stern, the acquaintance of many prominent German-Americans and subsequently con-

---

[17] *Milwaukee-Sonntagspost,* April 25, June 20, 1915; *Mitteilungen,* September, 1914, p. 12; April, 1916, p. 5. According to Richard Bartholdt (*From Steerage to Congress,* Dorrance, Philadelphia, 1931, p. 391), Lord Northcliffe "came over and bought, as he himself said, eighteen influential American newspapers." *Mitteilungen* for October, 1914, p. 5, declared: "Es ist leider eine Tatsache, dass eine ganze Reihe von amerikanischen Zeitungen auf englisches Kapital sich stützen. Daraus erklärt sich ihre Vorliebe für Alles, was englisch ist, und die infame Hetze gegen Deutschland. Daraus erklärt sich auch, dass so viele Engländer Stellen als verantwortliche Redakteure hierzulande bekleiden. Sie sind eine Gefahr für unser Land, da ihnen jeder wahre Patriotismus fehlt."

fessed that his reception in the state had given him considerable encouragement. The Alliance also arranged a propaganda tour for the Indian Nationalist leader, Naraban
Krishna of Bombay, whose presence in the United States was
considered evidence in itself of a flaw in the democracy for
which the Allies were said to be fighting.[18]

After the cutting of the German cable by the British navy,
Germany became dependent upon the two radio stations at
Sayville and Tuckerton for the communication of her news
to the United States. Many of the reports of German victory
which were daily spread across the front pages of the German-
language newspapers were gathered by this means. Hence to
the German-Americans these stations were of considerable
importance, and the Alliance seems to have made them its
special protégés. The fact that they were subject to censorship
by the United States Navy Department was found to be particularly irksome. On August 10, 1914, Hexamer wrote to the
secretary of state to complain that, while this censorship was
rigidly enforced, the British cable was allowed to go absolutely free from government supervision.[19] On August 20 a
request was made by Dr. Charles H. Weinsberg, president of
the Missouri Alliance, that in justice to both sides there be

[18] *Mitteilungen*, November, 1914, p. 20; December, 1914, p. 19; February,
1915, p. 21; September, 1915, p. 54; *Germania-Herold*, November 3, 14, 25,
1914; *Milwaukee-Sonntagspost*, June 27, 1915; *Milwaukee Sentinel*, December
12, 1914; November 23, 1915; *New-Yorker Staats-Zeitung*, November 25, 1915.
Between the end of September, 1914, and May 4, 1917, when he returned to
Germany, Kühnemann traveled 107,600 miles in the United States, spoke in
137 cities in 34 states and the District of Columbia, gave 121 speeches in
English and 275 in German, and was heard by about 213,580 people. See
Mitteilungen, June, 1917, p. 5. Dernburg, after his trip to Wisconsin, wrote
to Leo Stern: "Ich freue mich, in dem Bewusstsein weggegangen zu sein, dass
ich Ihrer aufopfernden Tätigkeit zu nützen in der Lage gewesen bin. Der
Empfang in Milwaukee hat mich zweifellos ermutigt." *Germania-Herold*, December 18, 1914. See also the issue for December 12.

[19] *Mitteilungen*, September, 1914, p. 7; *New-Yorker Staats-Zeitung*, August
22, 1914. At the same time the ambassadors of the Allied Powers protested
against the operation of the radio stations. It was claimed that they were
being used for military purposes (which, of course, the United States censorship was designed to prevent) and as such were contrary to the terms of the
Hague Convention of 1907, which forbade belligerents to operate radio stations for military purposes on neutral territory. *World*, August 18, 1914.

no censorship at all. This was supported by resolutions passed
by the Ohio Alliance on August 23, and by a telegram addressed to Wilson by the Illinois Alliance the next day. When,
on September 16, Tuckerton was disabled through an acci-
dent to its machinery, Hexamer charged that there had been
acts of sabotage, and urged Representatives Bartholdt of
Missouri and Donohue of Pennsylvania to press for an investigation by Congress.[20]

Any challenge thrown down by opponents of the German
cause was at once taken up by leading members of the Alliance. When a prominent Eastern churchman, the Reverend
Newell Hillis, declared that the German-Americans ought to
use their influence with the German government in the cause
of peace (a statement heartily commended by the *New York
Times*), Henry Weismann asked him to debate the whole
issue publicly, a challenge which Hillis declined. And when,
on January 27, 1915, federal judge John E. Killits said, at
Toledo, that although himself a German, "it was all the same
to him if someone showered a thousand bombs upon the
kaiser's head," the Cincinnati Alliance sent in vigorous protests to Washington.[21]

The nation's schools, urged the press bureau of the Alliance, should be carefully watched. For the teachers were dependent upon the Anglo-American newspapers for most of
their information, and were not prone to question all the
reports they read. The circular then added: "The hirelings of
England are not only to be found in the Senate and House of
Representatives, and in the press, but also in the churches and
schools. . . . The universities, too, must receive our attention. In some of them there are quite well-known teachers of

[20] *Westliche Post*, August 28, 1914; *New-Yorker Staats-Zeitung*, August 24,
1914; *Der Westen* (Chicago), September 6, 1914; *Germania-Herold*, September
18, 1914; *Mitteilungen*, October, 1914, p. 22; *New York Times*, September 17,
November 18, 1914. The station at Tuckerton was not reopened until November 17.
[21] *New York Times*, December 23, 25, 1914; *Mitteilungen*, March, 1915, pp.
25–26.

history who treat the war one-sidedly—namely from the stand-point of England."[22]

The war, indeed, found its way into more than one American university. In October, 1914, the Oregon Alliance discovered that the teaching in the state university was "completely on the side of the Allies," and therefore began to remonstrate with its president. Eliot of Harvard became the target of constant German-American abuse for his avowedly pro-British sympathies. According to the November, 1914, issue of *Mitteilungen,* he was "a dangerous demagogue, a man without true feeling of justice, and a partisan of the most lamentable kind."[23]

Wisconsin witnessed a remarkable demonstration of German-American susceptibility. One of her distinguished professors had published a "Graded French Method," in which certain exercises were alleged to be of an anti-German nature. The state Alliance was immediately up in arms. On January 18, 1915, Leo Stern, its president, protested that the book was a calumny of German family life and customs. In a somewhat unnecessarily abusive letter addressed to the president of the university he declared that the state Alliance, while eager to preserve academic freedom, objected strongly to "the appointment of men and women to the faculty of our University who are not mature enough to understand its meaning." On January 21 the Board of Regents appointed a committee of investigation, one member of which was also a member of the Alliance. The result was a complete victory for the Alliance, for when, on March 8, the committee issued its report, it offered not only an apology but also a promise that the offending passages would be removed from subsequent editions of the book.[24]

[22] *Milwaukee-Sonntagspost,* October 18, 1914. See also the article, "Scharfe Kontrolle der Schulen nötig," in *Mitteilungen,* November, 1914, p. 8.

[23] Page 9.

[24] *Germania-Herold,* January 9, 19, 21, March 8, 1915; *Mitteilungen,* February, 1915, p. 27; April, 1915, pp. 19–20.

A somewhat similar incident occurred in Indiana. Early in 1915 Professor Samuel B. Harding of the University of Indiana added a chapter on the European war to a textbook he had written. To this the Alliance objected violently. In a letter of March 27, 1915, to Harding's publishers it characterized the book as "obnoxious" and threatened "actively to oppose the use of such a book in any school anywhere in any state." The penalty for not removing or amending the offensive chapter was to be "a boycott, not merely as to the particular book, but all other books of that company." In view of the many positions on school boards and other educational bodies held by members of the Alliance, this was in reality a very powerful threat.[25]

After Eliot, Charles William Dabney of Cincinnati was to the Alliance the most hated of university leaders. The Cincinnati Alliance was among those which had followed carefully the injunctions of Hexamer to watch over the press and the public platform. On December 28, 1914, Dabney gave an address at Columbus, Ohio, in the course of which he denounced German imperialism and charged Germany with having begun the war. On February 5, 1915, the Cincinnati Alliance replied by drawing up resolutions demanding his removal, which it forwarded to the regents of the university and to the mayor of the city. A year later, in March, 1916, when Congressman J. Campbell Cantrill published in an interview a letter which he had received from Dabney urging him to stand firmly by Wilson against Germany, it again registered its displeasure. In a protest addressed to Dabney himself, and published in the press, it deplored his attempts "to foist his dangerous notions, personal fallacies, and national antipathies upon the community." The Cincinnati Alliance, the document proceeded, "considers such a procedure a presumption, deserving of signal and severest condemnation, by one who is merely a public servant, and as such

[25] Testimony of Harding in *Hearings on the German-American Alliance*, 620.

subject and subservient to public control. Hence the German-American Alliance of Cincinnati demands most energetically that either Dr. Charles W. Dabney desist in the future from similar agitatory acts, or that, in case of non-compliance, he be compelled to do so by the proper authorities."[26]

In his appeal of August 3, 1914, Hexamer had also asked all branches of the Alliance to institute collections for German war relief purposes. And when, on August 10, the first issue of *The Fatherland*, "a magazine devoted to fair play," appeared, it contained the following message from him:

At the recent serious time the duty of Germans and Americans of German ancestors of the United States is clearly defined. In the first place we must stand firmly united to safeguard the good German name against maliciousness and ignorance. I appeal to everyone of German birth or descent, high or low, rich or poor, capitalist, artisan, or working man, to take an interest in the agitation of the National German-American Alliance to create a two million dollar fund with which to aid the wounded and suffering.[27]

Accordingly many of the public meetings held in August resulted in the formation of permanent relief committees under the direction of the local Alliances.

There were high hopes as to the amount of relief work that might be undertaken. H. C. Bloedel of the Allegheny County Alliance of Pennsylvania reminded his fellow members of the million and a half dollars which had been raised during the war of 1870. *Mitteilungen*, like Hexamer, set the immediate aim at two million dollars, but the *Milwaukee-Sonntagspost* saw no reason why the ten-million mark should not be reached, if only wealthy German-Americans were willing to set aside one per cent of their incomes for this purpose. Actually nothing like this amount was ever realized, although the sums collected were considerable. By the end of January,

[26] *Brewing and Liquor Interests*, 2:2107–2109; *Mitteilungen*, March, 1915, p. 24; *Outlook*, 112:879–880 (April 19, 1916).
[27] *Fatherland*, vol. 1, no. 1, p. 13 (August 10, 1914).

1915, Pennsylvania, Wisconsin, and Ohio had raised $81,705, $67,276, and $35,584, respectively. From Milwaukee alone came $61,000. By January, 1916, the National Alliance had collected $600,000; by November, $800,000; and by March, 1917, when the work came to an end, $900,000—or just under one-fifth of the total amount from all German-American and pro-German sources.[28] The German and Austro-Hungarian ambassadors, to whom the money was handed over, continually expressed great satisfaction with the efforts that were being made. Bernstorff declared himself "strengthened more and more" in his "admiration for the extraordinary achievements of the National Alliance and its leaders," which would survive as "imperishable testimony to the sympathy of American citizens of German descent" for the cause of the fatherland.[29]

The money for relief purposes was raised in a multitude of ingenious ways. New York, Philadelphia, and other cities

[28] *Volksblatt und Freiheits-Freund*, August 11, 1914; *Mitteilungen*, September, 1914, p. 1; March, 1915, pp. 16, 18; "Richtlinien für die Sammlungen der Deutschen unter Aegide des Deutschamerikanischen Nationalbundes," in the *Milwaukee-Sonntagspost*, September 13, 1914. "The total sum remitted to Germany for our Red Cross and other similar societies amounts to over 20,000,000 marks," wrote Bernstorff in *My Three Years in America*, 139. The money was given to German and Austrian widows, orphans, war-wounded, and prisoners in England, France, and Siberia, German-American medical expeditions, the Turkish Red Cross, and the Irish Relief Fund. It is interesting to note that the Jews of Russian Poland—whose sad plight was so constantly bemoaned in the German-language press—were given only ten dollars of the eight hundred thousand dollars collected by November, 1916. See the list of disbursements in the *New-Yorker Staats-Zeitung*, November 29, 1916. According to Mr. von Bosse, the relief money never left the United States, but a corresponding sum was set aside for the stipulated purposes in Germany, and acknowledgments were always sent. Hence the charge, made in 1918, that the money had been employed by the German embassy for propaganda purposes. Statement to the writer, Philadelphia, October 6, 1937. A full summary of German-American relief work is given in Singer's *Jahrbuch*, 1918, pp. 204–271. See also *Mitteilungen*, January, 1915, p. 11; February, 1915, pp. 20–21; June, 1915, p. 8; July, 1915, p. 10; September, 1915, p. 16; December, 1915, pp. 19–25; December, 1916, p. 4; April, 1917, p. 4; *Milwaukee-Sonntagspost*, September 6, 13, 1914; January 23, 1916; *New-Yorker Staats-Zeitung*, August 17, 1914; February 28, 1915; July 1, 1916; February 28, 1917; *Hearings on the German-American Alliance*, 249, 265.

[29] Letter to John Tjarks, November 24, 1915, in the *New-Yorker Staats-Zeitung*, November 26, 1915. See also Bernstorff, *My Three Years in America*, 40.

formed, in October, 1914, a "Quarter" Club, each member
of which was pledged to contribute twenty-five cents a week.
The Wisconsin Alliance sold pictures of William II and
Francis Joseph. German-American women in Texas instituted
a *Nachthemden-Woche,* to make a thousand of the garments
suggested by that name. Tickets for the larger German-
American demonstrations brought in considerable amounts.
Leo Stern, in Milwaukee, auctioned a card of greeting which
he had received from Captain Paul Koenig of the *Deutschland,* the merchant submarine which paid so spectacular a
visit to the United States in July, 1916. A similar card, addressed to the German Societies of New York, sold for two
thousand dollars. The German War Veterans of New York
sold Iron Cross certificates, at a dollar and fifty cents, re-
spectively, for the first and second class. In many cities there
was kept a *Goldenes Buch* in which the German element
could record its devotion to the fatherland at so much per
page. And one rather unscrupulous collector was found, in
October, 1916, to be raising funds on the promise of titles of
nobility from the kaiser when the war was over.[30]

As in the days of Queen Luise of Prussia and the War of
Liberation, it became fashionable in some German-American
quarters to indicate one's devotion to the fatherland by wearing an iron ring. These rings, inscribed to resemble those
used during that earlier crisis in German history,[31] were

[30] *Mitteilungen,* October, 1914, p. 9; November, 1914, p. 7; *Germania-
Herold,* January 14, 1915; August 2, 1916; *New York Times,* October 23, 1916.
In connection with the sale of the Iron Cross certificates the New York
Kriegerbund founded a Bund des Eisernen Kreuzes deutscher Patrioten in
Amerika, under the patronage of Bernstorff. See the *Cincinnatier Freie Presse,*
February 11, 1915. Advertisers in German-language newspapers began to appeal to the German-American public through the fact that they were con-
tributing some of their profits to the German Red Cross. Thus one firm
offered its customers "die zweifache Gelegenheit . . . , dem Vaterlande zu
helfen und gleichzeitig einen Anzug für weniger als den halben Preis zu
kaufen." Advertisement in *New-Yorker Staats-Zeitung,* August 21, 1914.
[31] A common form of inscription read: "Dem alten Vaterlande / Die Treue
zu beweisen, / Gab ich in schwerer Zeit / Ihm Gold für dieses Eisen." *Fatherland,* vol. 2, no. 9, p. 30 (April 7, 1915).

distributed by the various branches of the Alliance in return
for gifts of jewelry or money. In some areas they were issued
in great quantities. Indiana, for example, in the first year of
the war, raised $2,437 by this means. The Delaware Alliance
distributed a hundred of them among its members at one
meeting in January, 1915, and Wisconsin, by the end of the
following month, had disposed of more than seven thousand.[32]

By far the greatest sums, however, were raised by means of
the *Wohltätigkeits-Basar*. Such bazaars were held in most of
the large cities at intervals during the war. They usually involved weeks of preparation, in which the local Alliances
cooperated with other German-American organizations, and
they lasted for several days. New York's first bazaar, of December 7–20, 1914, realized a profit of nearly a half million
dollars. Another, held in Madison Square Garden between
March 11 and 23, 1916, earned three-quarters of a million,
and was said to have received a million visitors. Other bazaars,
such as those held in St. Louis in October, 1915, and in Milwaukee, Philadelphia, and San Francisco in the spring of
1916, brought in correspondingly large amounts and inspired
columns of superlative description in the German-language
newspapers.[33]

When the British blockade brought stories of hunger in
Germany (many of which, however, were subsequently denied
in German circles), efforts were made to send food, in no
matter how small quantities, from the United States. On
March 10, 1915, Hexamer suggested that the parcel post
service might be used for this purpose. Any interference with
this service on the part of the Allies, he added, would constitute a *casus belli*. But all parcels were to be sent privately,

[32] *Mitteilungen*, February, 1915, p. 21; October, 1915, p. 18; *Germania-
Herold*, January 14, March 9, 1915. These rings were offered by a Birmingham,
Alabama, firm at the wholesale price of eleven cents each. When resold they
realized at least a dollar. *Mitteilungen*, February, 1915, p. 20.

[33] *New-Yorker Staats-Zeitung*, December 21, 1914; *Mitteilungen*, March, 1915,
p. 24; April, 1916, p. 23; *Westliche Post*, October 25, 1915; *Germania-Herold*,
March 3, 8, April 13, 1916; *Milwaukee-Sonntagspost*, May 14, 1916.

for any organized efforts would look like an agitation against the blockade.[34] On March 24 Postmaster General Burleson expressed the willingness of the post office to forward such packages "at sender's risk," but also gave notice that, so far as seizure was concerned, there could be no difference between parcel post and shipments by freight or express.[35]

The idea apparently became popular, for, according to the New York *World,* in four days six thousand packages were sent from Chicago alone, and merchants began to specialize in the making up of suitable shipments.[36] Particularly strong efforts were made to send condensed milk to the German babies. The difficulty came, however, on November 13, when the Holland-Amerika Line, which during the war had been carrying the American parcel post to Germany, notified the United States government that it could not accept this trade in the future. Immediately the Alliance began to agitate for the institution of an American-owned parcel post service to Germany, and Hexamer instructed all branches to make this demand of their congressmen. Wilson received petitions in its support from the state Alliances of Wisconsin, West Virginia, and Florida, and Carl L. Schurz and Bernard Ridder of the *New-Yorker Staats-Zeitung* went to Washington to plead with Burleson. The government announced that negotiations for a reopening of the service were pending, but in the end nothing was accomplished and the Alliance found itself compelled to abandon the scheme.[37]

To the extent of the various wartime activities which have been discussed in this chapter, the Alliance was very German: its members knew little restraint in their enthusiasm for the Central Powers. Entirely unnecessary were the exhortations of

[34] Such an agitation would presumably constitute an unneutral use of the United States postal system, and would therefore meet with resistance from the authorities. *New-Yorker Staats-Zeitung,* March 11, 1915; *Volksblatt und Freiheits-Freund,* March 12, 1915; *Mitteilungen,* April, 1915, p. 2.

[35] *World,* March 25, 1915.

[36] See the advertisement in the *New-Yorker Staats-Zeitung,* April 18, 1915, and in the *World,* March 25, 1915.

[37] *Mitteilungen,* December, 1915, p. 7; January, 1916, pp. 9, 18, 22–24.

German propagandists like Professor Kühnemann, who
warned them that, if Germany were defeated, they would
sink to the level of third-class citizens.[38] "Germany and
Austria are winning the war," rejoiced Henry Kersting, president of the St. Louis Alliance, "and to this result the German-
American Alliance, and above all the St. Louis Alliance, has
contributed its mite."[39] One prominent member of the
Alliance, the historian Ernst Bruncken, even regretted that
the German-Americans could not take a more direct part in
the conflict:

It is surely little enough that we Americans of German birth or
descent can do if we contribute mere money, although that is also
needed. From the standpoint of American citizens we ought to be
profoundly sorry that we are unable to take part in the tremendous sacrifices which are being made by the German people for
the preservation and welfare, first of their own country, and, as a
consequence, of all mankind. The true interests of humanity are
not dependent on material prosperity, such as we in America are
too apt to imagine the beginning and the end of patriotic en-
deavor. The true welfare of a nation is dependent upon ethical
considerations, and it is in the end a blessing rather than a
calamity for any nation to be called upon from time to time to
put forward its whole power and to sacrifice everything for an
idea, such as the Germans are doing today, and as this country
has not done since the glorious days of the Civil War.[40]

When so many eminent persons in the United States expressed strong sympathies for one set of European belligerents, it was hardly un-American for the Alliance to show such

[38] "Sie sinken dann zu verachteten Parias, zu Bürgen dritter Klasse herunter."
Article by Kühnemann in the *Milwaukee-Sonntagspost*, July 4, 1915. See also
the speech of Oskar Mezger, German consul at Cincinnati, in *Mitteilungen*,
October, 1914, p. 9.
[39] *Mitteilungen*, April, 1915, p. 15.
[40] Typewritten manuscript (F83614 AL) among the German-American pamphlets in the Wisconsin State Historical Library. The manuscript is a dupli-
cate of a letter to Victor Ridder, dated December 2, 1914. Bruncken, who was
assistant registrar of copyrights in the Library of Congress, was a member of
the Central Alliance of Washington, D. C. See, for example, a report of one
of his speeches in the *Cincinnatier Freie Presse*, August 14, 1914.

partisanship for the German cause. Very naturally, it stood whole-heartedly for the nation into which the majority of its members had been born, and whose culture it had originally been formed to diffuse. Its sympathy was ostensibly personal: for the German people, and the fathers and brothers of its members in the old world, and not for the German government. Yet there were many who expressed surprise at its attitude. It was expected to condemn German militarism and the invasion of Belgium. It was even expected to accept the thesis of Germany's war guilt expounded by her enemies. And when it refused to criticize German policy, certain people, by a strange turn of reasoning such as only the confusion of war could produce, began to perceive in its attitude the first proofs of disloyalty to the United States.

III

THE GERMAN–AMERICAN
ALLIANCE AND THE
MUNITIONS TRADE

AFTER AUGUST, 1914, THE ALLIANCE WATCHED THE GOVERN-
ment in its foreign diplomacy as carefully as it had been
watching it on the question of prohibition. At the beginning of the war there was considerable harmony between
the German-Americans and the president. Both set out with
a strong desire to keep the United States in a position of
strict neutrality. In his appeal to the nation of August 20,
Wilson urged every American to "act and speak in the true
spirit of neutrality, which is the spirit of impartiality and
fairness and friendliness to all concerned." He pointed out
that the people of the United States were drawn from "many
nations and chiefly from the nations now at war," and that
it would be "easy to excite passion and difficult to allay it."
Therefore, "the United States must be neutral in fact as
well as in name during these days that are to try men's souls.
We must be impartial in thought as well as in action, must
put a curb upon our sentiments as well as upon every trans-
action that might be construed as a preference of one party
to the struggle before another."[1]

These words were received with universal applause by
the German-Americans, who saw in them the promise of a
perfectly correct attitude on the part of the United States.
In the bulletin of the Alliance they were greeted with considerable warmth.[2] Branches throughout the country sent in

[1] The appeal is printed in the *Congressional Record*, 64 Congress, 1 Session,
vol. 53, pt. 14, appendix, pp. 523–524.
[2] "Der Präsident hat sich für die Dauer des Krieges eine Reihe von Ver-
haltungsmassregeln zurecht gelegt, die er streng einzuhalten gedenkt." *Mitteilungen*, October, 1914, p. 5.

telegrams to Wilson expressing their readiness to follow his neutral lead. According to the Houston Alliance, of Texas, no true American could deny the president his whole-hearted support.[3]

It was only as it became obvious that Wilson's injunctions were not being literally applied, and that in fact the administration itself was inclined to deviate from a strictly neutral course, that friction began to develop. A test case was the trade in munitions of war. To the prevention of this trade the Alliance, while protesting vigorously at every breach of American neutrality, devoted the greater part of its energies in the first year and a half of the war. Extremely conscious of the handicap under which the Germans suffered by reason of British control of the high seas, it pointed to the sale of munitions as a violation of that "spirit of neutrality" demanded by Wilson on August 20. If the United States was to be neutral "in fact as well as in name," it was not considered unreasonable to ask the government to forbid the trade altogether.

The manufacturers of munitions, however, were clearly less impressed by Wilson's appeal than the German-Americans. By the end of 1914, it has been said, the United States had become an "auxiliary arsenal" for the Allied Powers.[4] Millions of dollars' worth of war material, in the form of

[3] *Germania-Herold* (Milwaukee), October 1, 1914. See also the letter of Professor Julius Goebel to Hexamer in *Fatherland* (New York), vol. 1, no. 7, p. 14 (September 23, 1914), and *Germania-Herold*, September 8, 1914. For other favorable comment, see the *Milwaukee Free Press*, August 20, 1914; *New-Yorker Staats-Zeitung*, October 12, 1914; and *Cincinnatier Freie Presse*, October 12, 1914.

[4] Special Committee on Investigation of the Munitions Industry, United States Senate, *Munitions Industry: Report on Existing Legislation* (74 Congress, 2 Session, Senate Report 944, pt. 5, Washington, 1936). This document is hereafter cited as *Munitions Industry*. See also the statistics quoted by Richard Bartholdt in House Committee on Foreign Affairs, 63 Congress, 3 Session, *Exportations of Munitions of War: Hearings on H. J. Res. 377 and 378* (Washington, 1915), 29–32; Department of Commerce, *Statistical Abstract of the United States*, 1921, pp. 532–533; *Fatherland*, vol. 1, no. 14, p. 8 (November 11, 1914); vol. 1, no. 20, pp. 8–9 (December 23, 1914); *New York Evening Post*, December 14, 1914; *New-Yorker Staats-Zeitung*, April 21, 1915.

auto-trucks, horses, saddles, guns, and powder, had already been shipped to England, France, and Russia. Many manufacturers not normally engaged in this type of business had found it profitable to re-equip their factories to produce munitions. In many a northern city, at least one firm grew prosperous with the rush of Allied orders, and in some the bulk of the population, including German-Americans and even non-naturalized Germans and Austro-Hungarians (despite warnings of treason from their embassies),[5] had become economically dependent upon this trade in war supplies.

Against this ever-growing industry the German-American organizations, led by the Alliance and joined by pacifists who deplored the "Cult of the Dollar" at the peril of peace, and by a few economists who warned that the new prosperity was unsound, raised their voices in loud and vehement protest. In mass meetings throughout the country they expressed indignation that the United States should supply the weapons that killed their German kinsfolk, and remonstrated with the authorities for not acceding to the president's appeal.

The earliest war orders were furnished by Canada. Hence the Alliances of the border states kept a careful eye upon every shipment that left the country. Vigorous representations were made to the Department of State whenever these included materials of war. Thus as early as August 26, 1914, Hexamer forwarded to Washington a charge made by the Holyoke Alliance, of Massachusetts, that Colt's Armory Company was manufacturing machine guns for the Canadian government. An investigation was demanded, and it was asked whether this was not clearly a violation of American neutrality. Two days later he submitted a protest from the *Illinois Staats-Zeitung* against the sale of horses to the same government. The secretary of the Detroit Alliance, and of

---

[5] See, for example, the announcement of the Austro-Hungarian embassy threatening ten to twenty years imprisonment, and in some cases death, upon return to the Empire, to subjects who worked upon Allied munitions contracts in American factories. *Germania-Herold*, September 18, 1915.

the Erie Alliance of Pennsylvania, in September made similar protests against the huge consignments of coal that were being sent across the border—ostensibly for the fuelling of British battleships.[6]

To such protests the Department of State gave very discouraging replies. On September 11 Hexamer was informed, through Assistant Secretary John E. Osborne, that the administration found it inadvisable to impose restrictions upon its commerce in deference to the "divergent sympathies of the various elements of our population" when such restrictions were not warranted by international law and custom. In reply to the many representations received, the department decided, on October 15, to make public its position in a document entitled *Neutrality and Trade in Contraband.* Citizens of the United States, it was announced, could sell to a belligerent government or its agent any article of commerce they pleased. They were not restrained by any rule of international law, by any treaty provision, or by any statute of the United States. Their sales did not in the least affect the country's neutrality. If the articles sold were contraband of war, the enemy of the purchasing government had a right to prevent them from reaching their destination, but any inability to do so—as, in this case, through the British domination of the seas—imposed upon the neutral government no obligation to prevent the sale. "Neither the President, nor any executive department of the Government," the document concluded, "possesses the legal authority to interfere in any way with trade between this country and the territory of a belligerent. There is no act of Congress conferring such authority or prohibiting traffic of this sort with European nations."[7]

[6] *Volksblatt und Freiheits-Freund* (Pittsburgh), August 27, 1914; *Germania-Herold,* October 1, 1914; *Mitteilungen,* September, 1914, p. 20; October, 1914, p. 3. For evidence of the truth of the charge made by the Holyoke Alliance, see *Munitions Industry,* 12747.

[7] *Mitteilungen,* October, 1914, p. 20; *Congressional Record,* 63 Congress, 2 Session, vol. 51, pt. 16, p. 16814. On September 15 Bernstorff had submitted to

"We appealed to the spirit of the law, and you give us the letter," retorted George Sylvester Viereck, in *The Fatherland* of October 28. This document was indeed a severe blow to the hopes of the German-Americans. To them it was a condition and not a theory with which the United States was confronted. The very fact that the Central Powers were prevented from purchasing munitions meant that American neutrality, in its present form, was to the exclusive advantage of the Allies. And this was not neutrality in the sense of Wilson's own appeal of August 20. By conforming to the letter of the law rather than to the spirit the United States was really committing an act of manifest injustice, so the German-Americans felt, against the Central Powers. "Some of the greatest crimes of history," Hexamer later pointed out in a letter to the Senate Committee on Foreign Relations, "have been perpetrated behind a cloak of technical legality."[8]

It was obvious that mere protest was useless and that something more had to be done. In its document of October 15 the Department of State had unwittingly given a hint. Congress had never imposed a permanent embargo on arms to European belligerents—but why should it not be induced to impose one now? "It is Congress alone that can prohibit the export of absolute contraband of war," announced the press bureau of the Alliance, citing also the embargo on certain munitions to France in January, 1871, for which the Ger-

Lansing a list of Allied war purchases in the United States, adding, "I know that I cannot make any complaint in this matter, but I only wish to draw your attention to it." To which Lansing had replied: "I am glad to have this information, but, as I recently told you, there appears to be nothing that can be done to prevent traffic in contraband of war under the neutrality laws or the treaties of tht United States so long as such traffic is limited to ordinary commercial transactions by citizens of the United States." *Munitions Industry*, 103–104. It was not until later—in its reply of April 21, 1915, to the German note of April 4—that the administration took the stand that the imposition of an embargo would constitute a change of the rules of neutrality during the progress of a war, and therefore an act of unneutrality against the Allied belligerents. *Ibid.*, 14.

[8] *Germania-Herold*, February 6, 1915.

man-American lawyer, Louis Schade, had been to a great extent responsible.[9]

Hexamer had apparently given the problem serious reflection. On October 9 he proposed to engage two experts in international law to go to Washington and exert pressure upon Congress. At the same time he communicated with Richard Bartholdt, whom a recent report in the bulletin of the Alliance, perhaps to his embarrassment, had called "the most German of all Congressmen." At the end of November there came news that Charles M. Schwab had negotiated a fifty-million-dollar contract in Europe, and something had to be done immediately. Hexamer had already found one lawyer, E. Frank Carson, who in the Philadelphia *Public Ledger* had revealed the many inconsistencies of the existing neutrality of the United States, and it was decided to entrust him with the case. Carson thus went to Washington on December 2 as the agent of the National Alliance. On December 10 he saw Bryan and presented him with his first complaint. This was to the effect that large cannon were being shipped over American railroads to Canada, and that submarines for the Allied Powers were being built in American ports. An investigation was promised.[10]

Hexamer himself dealt with the question at considerable length at a mass meeting in Philadelphia on November 24. In the course of his address he denounced the "lick-spittle policy of our country" toward Great Britain, and suggested that the United States should, as its national emblem, replace the stars and stripes with the dollar mark, and for *E pluribus unum* substitute "Get the dollar, no matter how you get it." A country, he added, which prayed for peace on Sunday and during the rest of the week supplied the Allies with arms,

[9] *Mitteilungen*, October, 1914, p. 21; *Germania-Herold*, October 1, 1914.
[10] *Mitteilungen*, August, 1914, p. 6; January, 1915, p. 13; *Volksblatt und Freiheits-Freund*, October 10, December 11, 1914; *Germania-Herold*, October 10, December 2, 1914; *Westliche Post* (St. Louis), December 11, 1914.

ammunition, and every other contraband of war, was "to say the least, hypocritical."[11]

Hexamer also sent a carefully prepared statement of the German-American position to Wilson. In this document, which reached the White House on the same day that Carson presented his memorandum to Bryan, he demanded that "the proclaimed neutrality" be observed "most strictly in deed and action." "You cannot imagine, Mr. President," he said, "with what chagrin and bitterness it fills the Americans of German descent to see the resources of this great country, which they have helped to build up, and in whose battles they have given their life-blood, placed at the disposal of enemies who, with their overwhelming forces have proclaimed it their avowed purpose to crush our ancestral home." Another meeting, called by the Alliance in Philadelphia on December 11, endorsed the letter "on behalf of 41,700 citizens" and drew up resolutions to be sent to all members of Congress. Copies of the letter were also forwarded to Carson and to Bartholdt, with the invitation to act thereon as they thought fit.[12]

Bartholdt, however, had already acted. On December 1 he and Congressman Henry Vollmer, president of the German-American Central Verein of Davenport and Scott County, Iowa, were the chief speakers at a mass meeting in Chicago. Here they both announced their intention of submitting bills to Congress to end the arms traffic. Six days later they introduced into the House two almost identical measures "to prohibit the export of arms, ammunition, and munitions from any territory or seaport of the United States." As Bartholdt later pointed out, these did not impose a direct embargo. To enhance their chances of success, they merely empowered the president to stop the exportation of arms

[11] The speech was also issued as a pamphlet. A copy is in the library of the State Historical Society of Wisconsin (F 83614).

[12] *Mitteilungen*, January, 1915, pp. 6, 7; *Exportations of Munitions of War*, 20–21; *Germania-Herold*, December 11, 1914.

and munitions, "thus leaving the matter entirely to his discretion."[13]

The next step was to make a show of support for the Bartholdt and Vollmer bills. There was no shortage of speakers to plead for them, for the Alliance mobilized its entire strength behind them. On December 30 a deputation appeared before the House Committee on Foreign Affairs, to which the bills had been referred. This was composed of the two congressmen sponsoring them and all the leaders of the Alliance who could get to Washington. Hearings took place on December 30 and 31 and January 4.[14]

Vollmer opened the proceedings at the first hearing by stressing the moral necessity for an embargo. An embargo would help to bring peace in Europe, and through peace the United States would ultimately enjoy greater prosperity than through war. As it was, the existing neutrality system was playing directly into the hands of the armament manufacturers and "building up in this country a very dangerous special interest" that might eventually use its power to divert the country from the path of peace "to the gory road of militarism." There was not a member of Congress present who was not conscious of the pressure exerted by "these contractors, this ammunition ring," through its subsidized press, upon both bodies of the national legislature.

Bartholdt followed with a denunciation of the "malignant dollar neutrality." He quoted precedents in support of an embargo. On April 22, 1898, Congress had empowered the president to prevent, at his discretion, the exportation of coal "or any other material used in war" from any seaport of the United States. And an act of March 14, 1912

[13] *Germania-Herold,* December 2, 1914; Singer's *Jahrbuch,* 1916, pp. 15–21; *Congressional Record,* 63 Congress, 3 Session, 52:12; Bartholdt, *From Steerage to Congress,* 369. Bartholdt was a Republican and Vollmer a Democrat. The two bills were House Joint Resolutions 377 and 378. Similar bills were introduced by Senator Hitchcock (S. 6688) and Congressman Lobeck (H. R. 19548).
[14] *Exportations of Munitions of War,* 9 ff. A German-American account of the hearings is given in Singer's *Jahrbuch,* 1916, pp. 63 ff.

(apparently regarded by the present administration as having repealed the preceding measure), had prohibited the exportation of munitions to "any American country where revolutionary conditions exist." The United States, Bartholdt insisted, was doing business with one group of European belligerents to the material detriment of the other. Every bullet exported might "cost the life of a German or an Austrian, citizens of friendly nations." "And yet these nations can claim the kinship of 25,000,000 Americans. That is where the trouble is. Do you wonder, then, at the growth of the movement which aims to put a stop to this business? These 25,000,000 people, representing probably 5,000,000 votes, are convinced that the United States is waging war against the two Germanic nations under the cover of neutrality . . . . Immense mass meetings have been and are being held in the large cities, and the interest manifested at these meetings exceeds anything witnessed since the Civil War."

Hexamer was the principal speaker at the session of January 4. Following up skilfully the arguments advanced by the two previous speakers, he hinted that the embargo might be made the basis of retaliation against British interference with American trade. He emphasized what he considered to be an antagonism between British naval policy and the neutral trade rights of the United States. He pointed out the illegality of British interference with American ships not carrying contraband of war, and suggested the appointment of a commission which, in collaboration with the Department of State, should decide what steps were to be taken to reopen non-contraband trade with the Central Powers. The value of an arms embargo as the instrument of such a policy should not be overlooked.

A group of other officers of the Alliance followed Hexamer. Theodore Sutro, now chairman of its legislative committee, reminded the government of Wilson's appeal of

August 20, in accordance with which the United States "should refrain from arming one nation against another." Alphonse G. Koelble, president of the United German Societies of New York, claimed that international law was merely the promulgation of a doctrine by one nation and its acceptance by another, and accordingly urged that "we should put upon the statute books the absolute law that at all times no manufacturing concerns can ship a dollar's worth of munitions or arms out of the United States."[15]

By this time the agitation had spread far beyond the House Committee on Foreign Affairs, and there was work to be done in a much broader field. Petitions in support of the embargo were coming in from all parts of the country, some of them spontaneous, but many more prompted by the Alliance and the German-language newspapers.[16] Huge bundles, said to contain the signatures of two million citizens, were wheeled into the Capitol at Washington. Mass meetings were held in most of the large cities, often with pro-German congressmen and state governors on the platform.[17] The German Evangelical Synod of North America telegraphed its support.[18] In Wisconsin the Alliance was assured of the support of six congressmen and of Senator La Follette, and in the state legislature a German-American

[15] *Exportations of Munitions of War*, 9–12, 17–21, 49–53, 59, 69. Other statements urging such an embargo followed from Dr. Charles H. Weinsberg, president of the Missouri Alliance; John B. Mayer, president of the Central Alliance of Pennsylvania; the Reverend Georg von Bosse, pastor of St. Paul's Lutheran Church, Philadelphia (father of the Reverend Siegmund G. von Bosse, who later became president of the Alliance); and James B. Clark, president of the United Irish Societies of America. See also Georg von Bosse, *Ein Kampf um Glauben und Volkstum* (Belsersche Verlagsbuchhandlung, Stuttgart, 1920), 240.

[16] *Mitteilungen*, February, 1915, pp. 14–15; *Fatherland*, vol. 1, no. 25, p. 12 (June 27, 1915). See the specimen letters to Congress in the *Illinois Staats-Zeitung* (Chicago), January 4, 1915.

[17] For example, Governors Brumbaugh of Pennsylvania and Colquitt of Texas. See the *Germania-Herold* for February 1, 1915, and *Fatherland*, vol. 2, no. 2, p. 7 (February 17, 1915). Horace L. Brand, one of the sponsors of the embargo movement in the Middle West, told a Chicago audience on February 7, 1915, that demonstrations had been held in thirty-five cities in twenty-three different states. Singer's *Jahrbuch*, 1916, pp. 69 ff.

[18] *Germania-Herold*, December 21, 24, 1914; February 2, 1915.

member introduced a resolution memorializing Congress
to accede to the embargo. A similar resolution was also introduced into the state legislature of Iowa.[19]

Meanwhile certain Irish organizations had shown themselves willing to follow the German view of American neutrality. The result was the formation of Neutrality Leagues
in Philadelphia, Chicago, Milwaukee, and St. Louis. The
backbone of these was usually the local branch of the Alliance, and it became the ultimate aim of the latter to have
them in all of the large American cities. "Carry the agitation into American circles," urged *Mitteilungen* of February, 1915; "set up a Neutrality League in every locality, with
Americans at the head, so that these, in addition to the German societies and congregations, can send in their petitions
to Washington."[20]

On January 30, 1915, the supporters of the embargo movement met in conference, under Bartholdt's leadership, at the
New Willard Hotel in Washington. "Break away from England," was the watchword of the fifty-eight delegates who attended. These represented every large German-American
organization and every shade of pro-German opinion. The
Alliance sent its president, Hexamer; the German-language
press, Victor and Bernard Ridder of the *New-Yorker Staats-
Zeitung*, George S. Viereck of *The Fatherland*, Emil von
Schleinitz of the *Germania-Herold*, Horace L. Brand of the
Illinois Staats-Zeitung, and Max Heinrici of the press bureau of the Alliance; the Evangelical Lutheran Church of
North America, the Reverend G. C. Berkemeier; the Central Verein, Joseph Frey; and the "pro-Germans," Congress-
men Vollmer, Barchfeld, Bartholdt, Lobeck, and Porter, Dr.

[19] *Milwaukee Sentinel*, January 28, 1915; *Germania-Herold*, January 25,
27, February 4, 1915; *Illinois Staats-Zeitung*, January 20, 1915. The Wisconsin
resolution, which was greeted with considerable enthusiasm in the German-
language press of the state, passed in committee, but was defeated in the Senate
after a long debate. See *Germania-Herold*, March 4, 1915. The Iowa resolution
was also defeated.

[20] *Mitteilungen*, February, 1915, p. 14.

Thomas C. Hall, and Professors William R. Shepherd and James T. Hatfield.[21]

Washington, according to the New York press, was taken completely by surprise. Official circles were "puzzled" at the sudden growth of so formidable a movement. There was talk of a "German lobby" and of a "pro-German plot" in American politics. The *Literary Digest* registered "grave misgivings" in many quarters. In the opinion of the *New York Times,* the *Sun,* and the *Evening Post* it was the work of "German agents," while to the *Brooklyn Eagle* it bore "a close resemblance to treason."[22]

The conference lasted only a day. After a somewhat animated debate as to whether it should be satisfied with a mere declaration of principles or proceed with the establishment of a permanent organization, it finally agreed to have both. To many of the delegates it was a mere show of strength in favor of the arms embargo, but there was no lack of enthusiasm for the new organization, which emerged in the form of an American Independence Union. This, it was felt, should be led entirely by men "of Anglo-Saxon lineage" (to disguise its pro-German nature), but in the end it decided to have the German-born Bartholdt as its presi-

---

[21] *New-Yorker Staats-Zeitung,* January 31, 1915; *Milwaukee-Sonntagspost,* January 31, 1915; *Volksblatt und Freiheits-Freund,* February 2, 1915; *World* (New York), February 2, 1915. Bartholdt, *From Steerage to Congress,* 369 ff. Carl Wittke in his book *The German-Americans and the World War* (Ohio Historical Collections, vol. 5, Columbus, 1936) refers to this conference on three occasions (pp. 61, 64, 83–86), in such a way as practically to leave the impression—utterly erroneous, of course—that there were three such conferences.

[22] Quotations from the *Literary Digest,* 50:299–301 (February 13, 1915), and the *World,* February 2, 1915. See also *Fatherland,* vol. 2, no. 1, p. 1 (February 10, 1915); *Nation,* 100:133–134 (February 4, 1915); also charges made by Maurice Leon in an open letter to Chairman Henry Flood of the House Committee on Foreign Affairs, in the *New York Herald* and *Sun,* February 8, 1915; and Bartholdt's defense in the *Congressional Record,* 63 Congress, 3 Session, 52:267. Much was made in the press of the refusal of Dr. Kuno Francke, German-born head of the Germanic Museum at Harvard University, to attend the conference. See the *Independent,* 81:255–256 (February 22, 1915) and the *American Review of Reviews,* 52:89–90 (July, 1915). Francke, however, showed a tendency to be recklessly pro-German in 1917. See below, pages 164–165.

dent.[23] The declaration of principles, the last of which, according to the New York *World* (which was now giving great attention to the German-Americans), "contained the sting" of the whole conference, was as follows:

Whereas: the shipment of arms, ammunition, and munitions of war under conditions now prevailing is unfair, unneutral, and in violation of America's ethical ideals; tends to prolong the war; and is irreconcilable with our prayers for peace . . .

Therefore: in order to re-establish genuine American neutrality, to uphold it free from commercial, financial, and political subservience to foreign powers, be it

Resolved: that we, citizens of the United States, agree to effect a national organization, the objects and purposes of which may be stated as follows . . .

We favor, as a strictly American policy, the immediate enactment of legislation prohibiting the export of arms, ammunition, and munitions of war . . .

We pledge ourselves, individually and collectively, to support only such candidates for public office, irrespective of party, who will place American interests above those of any other country. . . .[24]

The Washington conference was carefully timed. It immediately drew public attention to the Bartholdt and Vollmer bills, and to the large bulk of German-American and other opinion behind them. The daily press took particular notice of its proceedings. The German-language newspapers hailed it with an outburst of enthusiasm; it was "true independence" and "the spirit of 1776." It had, moreover, threatened political disaster to all who opposed the embargo. A

---

[23] *Milwaukee-Sonntagspost,* January 31, 1915; *New-Yorker Staats-Zeitung,* February 21, 1915. The delegates from the Alliance made a particularly determined stand against having German and Irish names at the head of the organization. See the *Milwaukee-Sonntagspost,* January 31, 1915. This position, however, was vigorously attacked in an English editorial in the *Illinois Staats-Zeitung* (February 2, 1915): "We strongly oppose any admission by which our parentage could be used in the future as an argument that our patriotism is of an inferior order compared with that of those bearing English names."
[24] *World,* February 2, 1915; *Fatherland,* vol. 2, no. 1, p. 4 (February 10, 1915); Singer's *Jahrbuch,* 1916, p. 64.

powerfully organized German vote might send to Washington a Congress of a very different complexion in 1916, if the measure did not go through in the present session. "One hundred and seventy members of Congress are of Irish extraction," wrote Viereck in *The Fatherland;* "there is no reason why they should not be joined by one hundred and seventy of German extraction." [25]

Bartholdt did not hesitate to remind his colleagues in the House of Representatives of the support which the embargo had gained. In a speech of February 19, which was greeted with prolonged applause, he pointed to the many shades of American opinion which had been represented at Washington three weeks before, and to the general insistence upon "the observance of a strict and genuine neutrality as defined by all American Presidents from George Washington to Woodrow Wilson." The German-Americans, he told the House, were stirred as they had never been stirred before. Their state of mind manifested itself in great mass meetings and in the many petitions addressed to Congress in favor of an embargo. [26]

Would Congress accede to an embargo? There were whisperings that the measure was sure to pass, [27] and the German-Americans were confident of success. Before the House committee they had had the floor to themselves, and several members of the committee had even expressed their approval and had promised to vote for the Bartholdt and Vollmer bills. No representative of the armament interests

---

[25] *New-Yorker Staats-Zeitung,* January 31, February 22, 1915; *Germania-Herold,* February 1, 1915; *Fatherland,* vol. 2, no. 1, pp. 10–11 (February 10, 1915). "Schwer wie der Kampf ist, muss er im Interesse des Landes, dem wir Treue geschworen haben, gekämpft werden," wrote the editor of the *New-Yorker Staats-Zeitung,* February 1, 1915.

[26] *Congressional Record,* 63 Congress, 3 Session, 52:4126–4127. See also Bartholdt, *From Steerage to Congress,* 369.

[27] See, for example, the statement of Congressman Barchfeld to a reporter of the *Milwaukee-Sonntagspost,* at the Washington conference, "dass er schon aus politischen Gründen, die ich hier nicht näher kennzeichnen kann, mit absoluter Sicherheit auf die Annahme des Waffen-Embargo rechnet." *Milwaukee-Sonntagspost,* January 31, 1915.

had appeared to voice an objection. The press alone had tried to raise a scare against "the agents of Germany," but even then had not dared to defend the munitions trade.[28]

But the possibility of official pressure could not be entirely overlooked. The whole proceedings had been something of a challenge to the administration. As soon as the bills had been presented, in December, it was rumored that Wilson was considerably "annoyed" at those persons who, as he was alleged to have said, wanted to help him take care of American neutrality, but whose help had never been solicited.[29] However strong his humanitarian principles and his desire to bring about peace in Europe, the president was clearly unmoved by the appeals of the German-Americans. With the publication of Bryan's reply to Senator Stone of January 20, in which the secretary of state took considerable pains to stress that it had "never been the policy of this Government to prevent the shipment of arms or ammunition into belligerent territory, except in the case of neighboring American Republics," it became obvious that the administration would stand firmly by the absolute legality and correctness of the munitions trade. And this was not so much out of sympathy with the Allies, as the German-Americans were by this time beginning to assert, but chiefly perhaps because neither this administration, nor any other, could take the risk of destroying a trade which had become so largely the basis of American prosperity.[30]

[28] Bartholdt, *From Steerage to Congress*, 369. See also the "Report of the Committee which visited Washington, D. C.," in *Der Westen* (Chicago), January 10, 1915.

[29] To which the editor of the *Germania-Herold* (December 16, 1914) replied: "Herr Wilson darf sich versichert halten, dass die Millionen von Deutschamerikaner . . . doch etwas mehr also nur 'annoyed' sind."

[30] Bryan's letter to Stone is in *Corespondence between the Secretary of State and the Chairman of the Committee on Foreign Relations* (63 Congress, 3 Session, Senate Document 716, Washington, 1915), 9. "If it came to the last analysis," wrote House to Wilson on July 22, 1915, "and we placed an embargo on munitions of war . . . our whole industrial machinery would cry out against it." Charles Seymour, *The Intimate Papers of Colonel House* (2 vols., Houghton Mifflin, Boston, 1926, 1928), 2:58. See also Charles Seymour, *American Neutrality, 1914–1917* (Yale University Press, New Haven, 1935), 8.

The outcome was that Chairman Henry D. Flood, of the House committee, himself a supporter of the administration and probably, as was later charged,[31] acting under some form of pressure from the president, decided to pigeon-hole the bills. Bartholdt and Vollmer now found themselves stale-mated. They could have forced a vote in the House by bringing in a motion to discharge the committee from fur-ther consideration of the bills. But many who would have supported the bills would have voted against this proceed-ing, and finally there was reluctance to demand a vote at all. It became apparent that a possible defeat in the House would make matters worse, for the munitions manufactur-ers would "be sure to point to it as an official sanction of their nefarious business."[32]

On May 7 the *Lusitania,* carrying more than five thou-sand cases of that ammunition which the embargo would never have allowed to leave the country, was torpedoed off the Head of Kinsale. Amid the outburst of violent anti-German feeling that followed, the German-Americans, as we shall see later, were thrown immediately upon the de-fensive. For a time there tended to be considerable con-fusion, and then, when their forces did rally again, they had to be directed toward the more pressing task of trying to keep the country at peace.

In the autumn of 1915, however, the fight against the munitions trade was renewed. The signal for further ac-tivity was the appearance of the Allied commission under Lord Reading and Basil Blackett to negotiate a billion-dollar loan in September, 1915. Unless the Allies obtained this loan they could place no more orders in the United

[31] By Bartholdt, at a meeting at Pittsburgh on May 9, 1915. He also said that three million petitions, in all, had been sent to Washington in support of the bills, and that he had made repeated demands for another meeting of the House committee, but all had been ignored. See the *Westliche Post,* May 12, 1915. The charge that the government used pressure to defeat the bills was also made by Congressman Stafford of Milwaukee. See the *Germania-Herold,* August 6, 1915. See also *Munitions Industry,* 30.

[32] Bartholdt, *From Steerage to Congress,* 371.

States; with the exhaustion of their present funds the munitions trade would cease. It thus became the business of the German-American Alliance and other organizations to prevent the Reading-Blackett mission from being a success. If steps could be taken throughout the country to stop the loan from being floated, the credit system of the Allies would be ruined and with it perhaps the entire munitions business.

On the question of loans to belligerents, as on so many other questions which conflicted materially with the "true spirit of neutrality" urged by Wilson in August, 1914, the administration made a complete *volte face*. On August 15, 1914, in reply to an inquiry by J. P. Morgan and Company, the Department of State pronounced loans to belligerents inconsistent with American neutrality.[33] This position was modified on October 23, when, in a private conversation with acting Secretary Lansing (which was later communicated to a group of New York bankers), Wilson made a distinction between loans and credits. Accordingly American bankers at once began to extend credits to Allied purchasers. By the summer of 1915 another modification became imperative. Up to August 1 the Allied governments had paid only $174,000,000 toward the $450,000,000 worth of contracts which they had placed through J. P. Morgan in this country. Toward the end of the month there occurred a rapid fall in the pound, and terror struck American exporters as they saw the purchasing power of their best customer about to disappear. The only way out was the establishment of a large Allied credit in the United States, and on August 21, 1915, Secretary McAdoo wrote to the president imploring his immediate approval.[34] The result was that the adminis-

[33] *Munitions Industry*, 13, 19. There had been loud German-American protests against a proposed loan by Morgan as early as August 15, 1914. *Volksblatt und Freiheits-Freund*, August 16, 1914; *Fatherland*, vol. 1, no. 2, p. 1 (August 17, 1914); *Mitteilungen*, September, 1914, p. 7.
[34] *Munitions Industry*, 61–64.

tration reversed its policy and sanctioned the flotation of the Allied loan.

By this time the futility of mere protests to the Department of State had become apparent. Hence the Alliance this time came forward with a more drastic program. On September 15 Hexamer issued to all state branches a memorandum denouncing the machinations of the "Money Trust" and the "Anglo-American finance combine." German-American depositors were warned of a "conspiracy" to rob them of their savings and insurance and were exhorted to protest to their bankers and insurance agencies against the appropriation of their money for Allied war purposes. Clearing houses were told to inform all banks to expect a run of German-American depositors if they participated in the loan. At the same time the Alliance withdrew its own funds from the Merchants and Mechanics Bank of Baltimore because it was suspected of favoring the loan.[35]

The idea was to promote panic, or at least sufficient uneasiness to prevent any large financial operation from succeeding. In the German-language press the deal was denounced as unsound, as well as unneutral, and every effort was made to raise a scare. Even before Reading and Blackett landed in the United States, the Union of German War Veterans had, on August 31, in convention at St. Paul, Minnesota, resolved that none of its members should do business with any bank which sold Allied bonds, or which discounted the bills of munitions manufacturers. On September 6 the Friends of Peace, an organization brought into existence, as we shall see, to take some of the sting out of the *Lusitania* affair, and an affiliate of the Alliance, condemned the loan as "dangerous to the financial interests of our people" and a "breach of law and neutrality."[36]

[35] *Mitteilungen*, October, 1915, p. 2; *Illinois Staats-Zeitung*, September 16, 1915.
[36] *New-Yorker Staats-Zeitung*, September 1, 1915; *Germania-Herold*, September 7, 1915. The following are some of the headlines which appeared, in

The lead given by Hexamer's memorandum of September 15 was followed all over the country. In the East, German-American financial institutions, such as the German-American Chamber of Commerce and the German-American Savings Bank of New York, mobilized all their power against the loan. City Alliances joined in the general threat of a run on any bank associated with it. The Alliance of Syracuse appointed a special committee of three to investigate the activities of the various trust companies and banks in the city. In Washington, D.C. an *ad hoc* organization was called into existence on October 2 to remonstrate with the leading bankers. At German Day celebrations, on October 7, the Central Alliance of Pennsylvania demanded a special session of Congress to deal with the whole question. And in the state of New York, according to an announcement made by Henry Weismann, six hundred German-American societies, representing sixty thousand members, had by this time protested to Wilson against the loan as a breach of American neutrality.[37]

Perhaps even more vehement was the opposition in the Middle West. Here the German Press Association, representing editors of Illinois, Iowa, Wisconsin, Minnesota, Nebraska, and South Dakota, in convention at Dubuque, declared itself in full accord with the stand taken by the Alliance. On September 17 the Milwaukee German-Americans called upon their fellow citizens to take action against "this detestable conspiracy against the welfare of our people." This loan, if once accepted, it was declared, would mean immediate American participation in the war. In St. Louis the Alliance appointed a committee to bring pressure to bear

English, in German-language newspapers: "America Boards a Sinking Ship," *Illinois Staats-Zeitung*, September 24, 1915; "Would you lend money to a gambler—especially to a gambler who has lost?" *Volksblatt und Freiheits-Freund*, September 15, 1915; "Why buy British bonds, when Confederate bonds are cheaper and just as good?" *New-Yorker Staats-Zeitung*, October 30, 1915.

[37] *New York Times*, September 14, 19, 21, 24, 1915; *New-Yorker Staats-Zeitung*, September 16, 19, 20, 1915; *Illinois Staats-Zeitung*, October 3, 9, 1915.

upon the city bankers. On September 18 the Illinois Alliance, "in the name of 30,000 members," sent Wilson a telegram denouncing the acceptance of the loan as a "crime against humanity" and stating that it "considered it a great injustice to take away from the American nation so large a sum of money, which could be used for the development of its own industry and commerce." At its annual convention at Peru, a week later, it threatened a boycott of any bank "which participated directly or indirectly in this robbery."[38]

At one time there was talk of bringing all German-American money together in an entirely new banking system. A protest meeting, held in New York on September 23, claimed to represent deposits to the amount of twenty million dollars. Investigations were made in various localities as to exactly how much German-American capital was available. In New York City the estimates rose to seventy-five million dollars. Why should not this money be made the basis of "a great public service bank"? "The opportunity is at hand for German-Americans to assert and put into action the new idea of financial democracy." The money that was being placed at the disposal of the munitions trade, Hexamer insisted at a mass meeting in Chicago on December 9, could be used for better purposes in this country. With that sum of money, at least ten thousand miles of railroad could be built, whereas all that England would get out of it was, at the most, twenty days of warfare.[39]

[38] *Westliche Post*, September 25, October 22, 1915; *Milwaukee-Sonntagspost*; October 24, 1915; *Germania-Herold*, September 18, 1915; Singer's *Jahrbuch*, 1916, pp. 285, 287–289; *Illinois Staats-Zeitung*, September 26, 27, 1915; *New York Times*, September 26, 1915.
[39] *New-Yorker Staats-Zeitung*, September 24, October 7, 1915; *Mitteilungen*, January, 1916, p. 7. By November 22, 1915, the American Truth Society claimed to have organized fifty million dollars' worth of deposits under a committee of one hundred depositors. Singer's *Jahrbuch*, 1917, p. 57.
Hexamer also petitioned Congress for an investigation into the methods by which the loan to the Allies was being raised, claiming that there had been a violation of the United States banking and insurance laws. *New-Yorker Staats-Zeitung*, December 10, 1915.

The effect of the German-American campaign was at once apparent. While failing to hold back credit to the extent of strangling the munitions business, it at least retarded subscription to the loan. The bulletin of the Alliance pointed to the cold reception which the Allied commissioners received in the country as a whole, and to the bodyguard with which they were obliged to protect themselves. In many cities the bankers were terrified at the prospect of a German-American run and refused to be associated with the loan. The good will of German-American depositors was often preferable to the commission offered by the Allied governments. The result was that "the market for the Anglo-French bonds was not good," and Britain and France had to spend huge sums buying them at par in order to keep up their price.[40]

On December 15, 1914, the German government had dealt a severe blow to the embargo agitation by admitting the legality of the arms trade at the very time when the Bartholdt and Vollmer bills were being submitted to Congress.[41] On the loans question it again gave away the German-American case. At the moment when the German-Americans called for a boycott of the Allied loan, subscriptions were invited in the United States to the third German loan, and the German-language newspapers that protested against the

[40] *Mitteilungen,* October, 1915, p. 3; *Munitions Industry,* 66. As a gesture to their German-American depositors, ten Milwaukee banks even offered to cease business with New York clearing houses which participated in the loan. See the *Germania-Herold,* September 16, 17, 1915. The National Bank of Commerce of St. Louis promised that it would reconsider its decision to participate in the loan. See the *Westliche Post,* October 5, 1915. According to John R. Rathom of the *Providence Journal,* as much as fifty per cent of the banking power in the United States was in German-American hands. Quoted in the *New York Times,* July 29, 1915. See also *ibid.,* September 17, 1915; *New-Yorker Staats-Zeitung,* October 24, 1915; *Hearings on the German-American Alliance,* 115.

[41] Bernstorff, *My Three Years in America,* 60–66. On January 5, during the hearings before the House Committee on Foreign Affairs, Chairman Henry D. Flood confronted Bartholdt with this German admission on the legality of the arms trade, much to the latter's obvious embarrassment. Bartholdt denied any knowledge of it. *Germania-Herold,* January 6, 1915.

Allied credits as unneutral carried advertisements offering a thousand Mark Imperial bonds at $210 each.[42] By the end of 1915 about ten million dollars' worth of these bonds had been disposed of here—not a very considerable amount in the light of war-time finance, yet sufficient to enable the anti-German press to jibe at the inconsistencies of the German-American position.[43]

By the end of 1915 it was clear that the agitation of the Alliance and other German-American organizations against the munitions trade had failed. Despite every effort that had been made, an aggregate of $1,276,560,820 worth of Allied contracts had been placed in the United States, from which the firm of J. P. Morgan and Company alone had drawn a commission of nearly $13,000,000.[44] Too large an investment was thus at stake for the trade to be interfered with. For what, at any other time, might have been regarded as a sincere expression of patriotism, the German-Americans found themselves denounced, and their loyalty questioned, by the pro-Ally press. They in turn were becoming convinced that the Wilson administration was largely the tool of the "Money Trust," and were beginning to look to the election of 1916 as a chance of setting American government right again.

[42] On the very same page, for example, that it published the resolution of the Friends of Peace, passed at Chicago on September 6, 1915—"Wir erachten die Unterbringung von Kriegsanleihen für eine Gefährdung des Friedens."— the *Illinois Staats-Zeitung* bore the notice: "Neue deutsche Kriegsanleihe ausgegeben zu 99, 5% Zinsen tragend, Preis $210 für 1,000 Mark Bond." *Illinois Staats-Zeitung*, September 7, 1915. See also the *Germania-Herold*, September 10, 1915; *Milwaukee-Sonntagspost*, September 26, 1915.

[43] *Munitions Industry*, 61–63; Bernstorff, *My Three Years in America*, 83. The *New York Times*, on September 20, 1915, pointed out that "the opposition of German interests to the Allied loan goes hand in hand with the sale of German bonds."

[44] *Munitions Industry, Supplemental Report* (74 Congress, 2 Session, Senate Report no. 944, pt. 6), 66.

IV

THE FEUD WITH WILSON

ALL THROUGH THE YEAR 1915 THERE HAD BEEN DEVELOPING a bitter animosity between the Alliance and Wilson. The president's stand against the arms embargo and his change of policy on the loans question were but two of many instances of his partiality toward the Allies. In his diplomacy, too, he was regarded in German-American circles as having been unneutral. For while he had shown considerable severity in his dealings with Germany, he had allowed the British to violate American rights with impunity. It was, indeed, widely argued that by failing to assert the legality of American trade in non-contraband goods with the Central Powers, and by permitting the British navy to intercept American mail, and often American passengers, going to German ports, he had even sacrificed fundamental American interests to make the war easier for Great Britain.

Recent revelations of American policy during the war have tended to justify the German-American lack of confidence in Wilson's neutrality. According to one account, "Wilson, House, and Lansing, from the outset of the war, were convinced that, in the interests of the United States in particular, and of civilization in general, a German victory could not be permitted." The administration was "strongly pro-Ally in sympathy" and "almost never neutral in spirit." Wilson "was convinced that, fundamentally, American and British aims were similar," and this, of course, a long time before the United States entered the war.[1]

[1] *Munitions Industry,* 45, 55. This account, written by Miss J. J. Burns for the Nye Investigation, is not necessarily unbiased. But it has a very complete documentary basis, and is substantiated by what Lansing himself has left on record in his *War Memoirs* (Bobbs-Merrill, Indianapolis and New York, 1935).

German-American petitions to the White House seemed invariably to fall upon deaf ears. The first rebuff came very early in the war. On September 16, 1914, there arrived in the United States a Belgian commission, under the leadership of Minister of Justice Carton de Wiart, to solicit the sympathy of the American government. When it was announced that this commission would be received by the president, a delegation of German-Americans from Illinois, Indiana, and Wisconsin, led by Horace L. Brand of the *Illinois Staats-Zeitung*, also demanded a hearing, in order to state the German point of view. Wilson, however, refused to see the German-Americans, while receiving the Belgians with every courtesy. After this his plea for neutrality seemed to have a ring of insincerity in certain German-American circles, and Brand, who was one of the most powerful press men in the Middle West, became henceforth his bitter enemy.[2]

If every communication received by Wilson during the first eighteen months of the war has been carefully preserved, one bulky section of the presidential archives must bear witness to the constant interest, and not infrequent indignation, of the German-American Alliance. For during that period its various branches sent in to Washington many thousands of telegrams and petitions. These concerned almost every international issue that arose. Rarely, however, did they meet with a favorable reception, and in the end they merely tended to increase the bad feeling on both sides. Wilson showed irritation at the persistence of the German-Americans, and they in turn became more and more conscious of his determination to ignore them.

In the early stages of the war the government tended to

[2] *Milwaukee-Sonntagspost*, September 20, 1914. This particular report is from the press bureau of the National Alliance, which shows that the latter, although not directly responsible for the Brand mission, was watching it with interest. Singer's *Jahrbuch*, 1915, pp. 89–90; *World* (New York), February 2, 1915.

exasperate the German-Americans by not showing more concern over the intervention of Japan on the Allied side. On August 15, 1914, Hexamer warned the country of the dangers of Japanese aggression in the Far East. "Commerce in the Far East," he said, "will be annihilated, and the Pacific Ocean turned into a 'Yellow Sea.' Can the United States allow that? Can our country stand by complacently and see the Japanese join in the destruction of Germany so that as the next step, strengthened and confident of victory, they may turn against the United States?"[3] Three days later he appealed to Wilson to demand that "in the name of humanity, civilization, and world peace" Japan desist from further military operations. The Oregon Alliance even asserted that, in view of the Japanese danger in the Pacific, every German-American should join the National Guard for the defense of the United States. And on August 23, the day on which Japan officially declared war upon Germany, the Ohio Alliance drew up resolutions expressing grave concern over the Japanese seizure of Kiao Chau and indicting Great Britain for building up Japanese military and naval power at the expense of the United States. Copies of these resolutions were sent to the president, the secretary of state, and members of Congress.[4]

When in the succeeding months the administration seemed to maintain an attitude of considerable indifference toward Japan, German-American protests became frequent and vehement. "Weak-kneed" was the description of the government used by the Central Alliance of Pennsylvania at its annual convention at Lancaster on May 8, 1915. On August 24 the Milwaukee *Germania-Herold* denounced the policy of promoting, through the munitions trade, the cause of Japan at the expense of Germany, as "suicidal folly" and

---

[3] *Volksblatt und Freiheits-Freund* (Pittsburgh), August 16, 1914.
[4] *Mitteilungen*, September, 1914, pp. 23, 24; October, 1914, p. 20; *Volksblatt und Freiheits-Freund*, August 19, 1914; *New-Yorker Staats-Zeitung*, August 24, 1914.

a "crime against the white race." Some day the United States itself would be faced with a hard problem of defense, the bulletin of the Alliance predicted in December, if the entente between "unprincipled John Bull" and "land-hungry Japan" persisted.[5]

The incident which did most to widen the breach between the German-Americans and the administration in questions of foreign policy was the sinking of the *Lusitania*. On May 8, the day that the news of the disaster arrived, Hexamer and other officials of the Alliance were attending the convention of the Pennsylvania branch just mentioned. Plans had been made for a large membership drive during the spring of that year. Leo Stern of the Wisconsin Alliance was also in the East, where he had been with Dernburg, Bernstorff, and Hexamer, and discussed various aspects of German-American policy.[6] Contrary to all the stories of rejoicing circulated at the time,[7] the news of the disaster came as a great blow to the hopes of the German-Americans. According to Bernstorff, they were "terror-stricken by its violence," and there was perhaps little exaggeration in the words with which, on May 17, he informed the German government that "our propaganda in this country has, as a result of the *Lusitania* incident, completely collapsed."[8]

Most disturbing was the outburst that followed in the anti-German press. "Modern history," declared the New York *World,* perhaps the most vehement of all the large dailies, "affords no other such example of a great nation running amuck and calling it military necessity." "Can the

---

[5] *Volksblatt und Freiheits-Freund,* May 10, 1915; *Germania-Herold* (Milwaukee), August 24, 1915; *Mitteilungen,* December, 1915, p. 18.

[6] "Manche Angelegenheiten in Bezug auf die Aufgaben, die das Deutschamerikanertum noch zu erfüllen hat, wurden in längeren Gesprächen erörtert." Stern's report in the *Germania-Herold,* May 8, 1915.

[7] "Stories that groups in German-American restaurants had broken into cheers at the news and drunk toasts to the U-boat commander and sung 'Deutschland über Alles.'" Mark Sullivan, *Our Times: The United States, 1900–1925* (Scribners, New York, 1926–1935), 5:122.

[8] Bernstorff, *My Three Years in America,* 25–26, 121.

President of the United States save Germany from Germany?" "Does Germany want more war?" it asked in one editorial after another. After the first exchange of notes between Washington and Berlin, it added: "We are going to have international law, and not Prussian law, at sea. We are going to have international law, not in part but in its entirety. We are not going to bargain with Germany for this right. The bullies of Berlin have retreated halfway. They are going to retreat all the way."[9]

For a time the Alliance was thrown completely on the defensive. Assurances of loyalty were sent in to Washington from all parts, the Rochester Alliance of New York even pledging itself to the "unqualified support of President Wilson in whatever action he takes."[10] But this did not prevent it from being the target of considerable anti-German feeling. Hexamer had to answer a number of insinuating questions by newspaper reporters. One of his visitors was an *agent-provocateur,* who, "upon instructions from London," as the *Milwaukee-Sonntagspost* alleged, informed him that German-American volunteers were assembling for an invasion of Canada, and invited him to lead them. Threatening letters came into his office from all parts of the country. Later in the summer, when he was visiting the state of Washington, the mayor of Tacoma advised him not to enter the city because of the anti-German feeling there. John B. Mayer, president of the Central Alliance of Pennsylvania, and other prominent officials also complained to the police that they were being constantly pursued and watched by private detectives.[11]

To the German-Americans it was incomprehensible why

[9] *World,* May 8, 9, 10, 11, 12, 1915.

[10] *New York Times,* May 14, 1915. See also the expressions of loyalty in the *Literary Digest,* 50:1262–1264 (May 29, 1915), and "Back to the Fold," in the *Nation,* 100:589–590 (May 27, 1915).

[11] *Milwaukee-Sonntagspost,* May 23, August 29, 1915; *New-Yorker Staats-Zeitung,* May 24, 1915. An invasion of Canada was actually discussed in Germany as an opportunity for German-Americans to fight for the fatherland. See below, page 178.

Germany alone should be held responsible for the *Lusitania* tragedy. The German embassy in Washington, the German-language press pointed out, had warned passengers on British boats that they were entering a war zone. On May 3, four days before the sinking, the Milwaukee *Germania-Herold,* in a remarkably prophetic article, had argued the right of the German submarines to sink the vessel on its present voyage.[12] The British Admiralty had failed to provide it with adequate protection. In addition, it was carrying a contraband cargo of more than five thousand cases of ammunition.[13]

Hence the Alliance demanded a public inquiry as to where the real responsibility lay. On May 9 the Missouri Neutrality League, an outgrowth of the state Alliance, held a special meeting at which it expressed regret that the warning which Wilson had given to Americans in Mexico had not been extended to those traveling on British ships, and asserted that there would have been no such submarine warfare if the United States had enforced its right to sell foodstuffs to Germany. The demand for an investigation was pressed by the Wisconsin Neutrality League in a letter to

[12] This article, bearing the title "Die Warnung des deutschen Botschafters," not only justified the sinking of the *Lusitania,* but even seemed to predict it— "Warum die deutsche Botschaft ihre Warnung gerade jetzt erlassen hat, das ist unschwer zu erraten. Während der letzten vierundzwanzig Stunden sind wieder fünf alliierte Dampfer den deutschen Unterseebooten zum Opfer gefallen. Man darf daraus schliessen, dass die deutsche Admiralität entschlossen ist, ihre Kampagne mit verdoppelter Kraft weiter zu führen. Vielleicht bereitet sie sogar einen grösseren Schlag vor. Es wäre zum Beispiel möglich, dass sie den Versuch machen will, einen der ganz grossen englischen Passagierdampfer abzufangen. Am Samstag ist die 'Lusitania' von New York abgegangen. Eine grosse Anzahl von Amerikanern soll sich an Bord befinden. Diese Amerikaner handeln sehr unvorsichtig. Die englische Reederei aber, welche sie als Passagiere mitnimmt, macht sich einer unverzeihlichen Gewissenlosigkeit schuldig, denn es ist ihr natürlich wohlbekannt, dass die deutschen Unterseeboote ein vollkommenes Recht haben, die 'Lusitania,' die wahrscheinlich mit gewaltigen Massen von Kriegsmaterial beladen ist, anzugreifen, ohne sich erst nach der Nationalität ihrer Passagiere zu erkundigen. Nun das amerikanische Publikum ist gewarnt. Die deutsche Botschaft hat ihre Pflicht getan. Die Amerikaner, welche diese Warnung in den Wind schlagen, tun es auf eigene Gefahr."

[13] "Rechtzeitig gewarnt" (headlines), in the *New-Yorker Staats-Zeitung,* May 8, 1915; "Munition die Hauptfracht," in the *Volksblatt und Freiheits-Freund,*

Wilson of June 3. In the issue of June, 1915, *Mitteilungen* dealt with the question at some length in an editorial entitled "Unsere Pflicht ist ruhiges Prüfen." In this it was argued that "the time for calm investigation, for intelligent judgment, and for a restrained manner of speaking has arrived for the people of the United States. They should turn to each other and ask whether our country has always done the right thing, and whether, as a result of its one-sided traffic in arms and munitions, it does not bear some of the blame for this tragedy of the sea, which we deplore from the depths of our hearts . . ."

Resolutions charging Great Britain with the sole responsibility for the *Lusitania* disaster began to pour in to Washington. In the opinion of the Alliance of Omaha, expressed at a meeting on May 10, "the fate intended for that vessel had been announced in advance," yet nothing had been done to protect it. A week later Hexamer endeavored to persuade the General Assembly of Pennsylvania to condemn the transportation of American citizens on ships carrying munitions of war. In June the bulletin of the Alliance published a speech by Bartholdt, in which he declared that the United States government should formally protest against the failure of the British Admiralty to safeguard the Americans on the *Lusitania*. It also gave considerable prominence to a statement of Richmond P. Hobson (otherwise bitterly hated as an advocate of prohibition) to the effect that the Cunard Company had received orders from the British authorities to let the vessel go to her doom, in the hope of thereby drawing the United States into the war.[14]

May 9, 1915; "5,417 Kisten Munition an Bord," in the *Cincinnatier Freie Presse,* May 8, 1915. Even the bitterly anti-German *World* asked (May 9, 1915), "Where was the British navy?" "What did Britain do to guard against the disaster? . . . How could the British Admiralty, short of criminal negligence, permit the Lusitania unwatched to pass through those dangerous waters into the trap that was set?" See also Thomas A. Bailey, "The Sinking of the *Lusitania,*" in the *American Historical Review,* 41:61 (October, 1935); *Munitions Industry,* 14.

[14] *Mitteilungen,* June, 1915, pp. 4, 12–13, 17, 24; July, 1915, p. 1; *Westliche Post,* May 10, 1915; *Germania-Herold,* June 4, 1915.

The German-Americans were thus firmly convinced of Britain's guilt. They could not, indeed, believe otherwise as they read the strongly worded editorials that appeared day after day in the German-language press, presenting the German view of the crisis with more precision than did the Germans themselves. The following memorandum, sent to Wilson from the Deutscher Klub of Kansas City, Missouri, and published in the June issue of *Mitteilungen*, is a fairly representative statement of their case:

Mr. President,

As the administration has requested the public to express its opinion on the sinking of the *Lusitania*, we take the liberty to comply with your request. After due consideration of all the facts of the deplorable incident, we have arrived at the conclusion that England, and England alone, is responsible for the loss of the lives of Americans. The *Lusitania* was a vessel belonging to a belligerent nation, loaded with ammunition of war, destined for a war zone that had been declared as such months ago. According to international law it was therefore subject to the risks of war. The presence of passengers belonging to a neutral nation on such a vessel cannot change its status in war. Our citizens had no business to board this steamer. They knew the danger and had been forewarned sufficiently. But if England accepted them as passengers, it was the duty of England to protect them within the zone of war. It is not the office of the American flag to protect English shipping. Without doubt England has utterly failed even to try to protect the ill-fated steamer. For this reason we urge our Government to ask England for an explanation of its neglect and for due reparation.[15]

Wilson's three notes to Germany, of May 13, June 9, and July 21, filled the German-Americans with grave apprehension. They saw in them evidence of what the editor of the Pittsburgh *Volksblatt und Freiheits-Freund* called "American saber-rattling." They felt that the administration was being unduly influenced by the bellicose tone of the anti-

[15] *Mitteilungen,* June, 1915, p. 12.

German press. By maintaining the questionable right of American citizens to travel on the ships of belligerents, the president was playing into the hands of the munitions merchants, who were only too glad to have such passengers present to protect their cargoes. So lamented the New York State Alliance in a resolution passed at its annual convention at Utica on July 24. It was regrettable, complained the German-American cotton-growers who formed the De Witt County Alliance of Texas, that the president had not shown equal zeal in defending the right of the South to sell its produce in German markets.[16]

Throughout the summer the German-Americans were haunted by the specter of war with Germany. That there was a definite drift toward war during these months, despite America's unpreparedness and the self-righteousness which made Wilson "too proud to fight," we may infer from a memorandum drawn up by Lansing on July 11, 1915, and now published in his *Memoirs:*

Germany must not be permitted to win this war or break even, though to prevent it this country is forced to take an active part. This ultimate necessity must be constantly in our minds in all our controversies with the belligerents. American public opinion must be prepared for the time, which may come, when we will have to cast aside our neutrality and become one of the champions of democracy.[17]

To the preservation of peace the Alliance bent every effort. On May 23, 1915, the Massachusetts branch approved the following statement and instructed its secretary to send copies of it to Wilson, the secretary of state, and all members of Congress from the state:

We refuse to recognize the possibility of a war with Germany. There will be no war if we stand united.
Now is the time to show our American patriotism.

[16] *Volksblatt und Freiheits-Freund,* May 13, 1915; *Mitteilungen,* August, 1915, pp. 15–16; September, 1915, p. 58.
[17] Lansing, *War Memoirs,* 21.

Let us keep our country to her course of peace and independence.

Let us refuse to consider what to do in case of war because we are determined that there shall be no war.[18]

The questionable nature of American neutrality, the president was informed by Jacob Frohwerk on behalf of the Alliance of Kansas, was responsible for the whole crisis, and "our national honor demands that our own hands be clean" before resorting to war. Leo Stern of Wisconsin bluntly demanded of Wilson, on June 3, that he refrain from any drastic action against Germany. He also sprang to the defense of Dr. Anton Meyer-Gerhard, whom Bernstorff sent to Germany to explain the American position on the *Lusitania* question, when he was charged by certain pro-Ally newspapers of having a suspicious connection with the German war ministry.[19]

What really relieved the situation considerably for the German-Americans (as, of course, for other protagonists of peace) was the resignation of William Jennings Bryan on June 9. Hitherto Bryan had been the object of more German-American opprobrium than Wilson. For his leanings toward prohibition had earned him the none too gracious epithet of *Der Traubensaftmann,* and at the end of April, 1915, the press bureau of the Alliance had suspected him of trying to make the drink question a national issue in the election of 1916. He had also been generally considered to be pro-Ally, especially since his daughter was the wife of a British officer. Every charge of unneutrality against the administration was pressed doubly hard against Bryan, and his famous reply to Stone of January 20, coming as it did at the height of the agitation against the munitions trade, had singled him out as the particular enemy of the German cause.[20]

[18] *New-Yorker Staats-Zeitung,* May 29, 1915; *Mitteilungen,* June, 1915, p. 3.
[19] *Mitteilungen,* June, 1915, p. 11; *Germania-Herold,* June 4, 16, 1915.
[20] *Milwaukee-Sonntagspost,* May 2, 1915; *Memoirs of Wm. J. Bryan,* by

On June 9, however, when he left the administration
rather than assume responsibility for the second *Lusitania*
note, Bryan underwent a complete metamorphosis. In the
eyes of the German-Americans he was now "a knight without
fear," as the editor of the *Illinois Staats-Zeitung* referred to
him. "One thing seems certain," wrote Viereck. "We have
misjudged Mr. Bryan." Telegrams of congratulation poured
in. "Keep up the good fight," urged the Alliance of Spokane,
Washington; "an overwhelming majority of the people is
with you." "Twenty-five thousand American citizens of German descent in Greater New York congratulate you heartily
on your patriotic stand," telegraphed Henry Weismann. "We
congratulate you that you have placed your conscience above
your office, which shows courage and loyalty to principle," was
the message of the California Alliance. The circumstances of
his resignation, it was added, would open the eyes of the
American people to the dangers of their statesmen showing
partiality in foreign conflicts.[21]

Two days later, in the knowledge that it was they, above
all, who were gravely concerned over the recent course of
events, Bryan issued an appeal to the German-Americans.
This appeal, which was given a prominent place in all the
German-language newspapers, was at once a recognition of
the anxieties with which the German-Americans were beset,
and an attempt to reconcile them to the Wilson administration. While taking considerable pains to vindicate the course
which the latter had hitherto pursued, Bryan completely misjudged the position of the German-Americans. For he looked
to them to exert some sort of pressure upon German
diplomacy: "Knowing that the President desires peace," he
said, "it is your duty to help him secure it. And how? By
exerting your influence to convince the German government

himself and his wife, Mary Baird Bryan (Winston, Chicago, 1925), 427–428;
Germania-Herold, December 22, 1914; *Wisconsin Staats-Zeitung* (Madison),
February 9, 1915.
[21] *Illinois Staats-Zeitung* (Chicago), June 10, 1915; *Fatherland* (New York),
vol. 2, no. 19, p. 10 (June 16, 1915); *Mitteilungen*, July, 1915, pp. 24, 28, 31.

of this fact, and to persuade that Government to take no steps that would lead in the direction of war."[22]

This suggestion was immediately repudiated by the German-American leaders. The German-Americans were acting as American citizens in this matter, asserted Frederick Franklin Schrader in *The Fatherland,* "not as agents of the German Government." "German-Americans consider it a still higher duty to influence our own Government," retorted Julius Mörsch, president of the Minnesota Alliance, in an interview given to the *World.* It might be news to Mr. Bryan, added John B. Mayer of the Pennsylvania Central Alliance, but the German-Americans were American citizens, just as he was, and not German subjects. "Or has he swallowed the idea of so many that the National German-American Alliance is an organization under the direction of the German Government?"[23]

It was obvious that if there was to be any understanding between Bryan and the German-Americans, he would first have to listen to them, and not they to him. Yet to have him in their camp would be an enormous asset: their plea for peace and for the use of a milder diplomatic tone toward Germany would be far more convincing if it came from the lips of the late secretary of state. On June 8 the United German Societies of New York resolved upon a mass demonstration for peace, and were soon joined in this intention by the United Irish Societies, the Star Spangled Banner Association, the German Catholic Federation, the Socialist Party of New York, and other anti-war organizations. Immediately after his resignation Bryan was approached by Henry Weismann and Bernard Ridder of the *Staats-Zeitung* to be the chief speaker. To the anguish of many administration supporters he readily consented.[24]

[22] *World,* June 12, 1915; *Germania-Herold,* June 12, 1915.
[23] *Germania-Herold,* June 12, 1915, which referred to Bryan's suggestion as "mindestens überflüssig"; *Fatherland,* vol. 2, no. 20, p. 8 (June 23, 1915); *Mitteilungen,* July, 1915, p. 4; August, 1915, p. 18.
[24] *New-Yorker Staats-Zeitung,* June 20, 23, 1915; *World,* June 24, 1915.

The demonstration, held in Madison Square Garden on June 24, was destined to be a landmark in the German-American pacifist drive against Wilsonian diplomacy. The immediate object was to impress the president and the pro-Ally newspapers that an overwhelming majority of the people were not in favor of war with Germany.[25] Much publicity was given to the occasion by the German-language press, as by the German churches and the various clubs and societies. On the East Side thousands of leaflets in Yiddish were distributed to advertise it. Boxes in the Garden sold for fifteen, twenty-five, and fifty dollars each. Besides Bryan the speakers were to include Congressmen Frank Buchanan, a member of the House Committee on Naval Affairs, and Henry Vollmer, Jeremiah O'Leary, and Hexamer.

The nature of the demonstration was clearly indicated in a long appeal published by Weismann, Bartholdt, O'Leary, and others in the *New-Yorker Staats-Zeitung* on June 18:

We are of the opinion that President Wilson has been deceived as to the real feelings of the nation, and that public opinion does not demand, as the press would have us understand, a severe policy against Germany—and one which must necessarily be accompanied by immense risks. We believe, on the contrary, that the overwhelming majority of the American people want peace and disapprove of all steps which could lead to its disturbance. We consider it our most sacred duty of citizenship to enlighten President Wilson on this point . . .

The demonstration was thus obviously intended for Wilson's benefit. But the meeting was to do more than enlighten him, for the appeal then proceeded to state that it would "demand the referring of the differences of opinion between the two governments to a court of arbitration." In other words, the German-Americans had so little faith in Wilson's diplomacy

[25] "Die Augen des Landes, ja der ganzen Welt, werden auf diese Versammlung gerichtet sein und Präsident Wilson dürfte aus ihrer Grösse und Begeisterung auf die wahre Stimmung unseres Volkes seine Schlüsse ziehen." Appeal of

that they would take the *Lusitania* question out of his hands entirely.

The demonstration was in every way equal to the expectation of its promoters. According to reports from the police authorities, seventy thousand persons tried to gain admission to the Garden, and four outdoor meetings had to be held to accommodate the overflow. Not since Bryan's appearance there during the campaign of 1900, even the bitterly hostile *World* was forced to admit, "had such a tide of humanity beat against its doors." According to that same newspaper, however, the proportion of German-Americans to others there was "fully nine to one."[26]

Two minutes of uninterrupted cheering greeted Bryan when Henry Weismann introduced him as "the new leader of the American people who stand for peace." So pleased, indeed, were the German-American leaders at Bryan's presence that at a dinner in his honor at Holland House before the meeting, they had been content to offer water as the only beverage, and had permitted the sale of small bottles of grape juice at the meeting along with their own *Kaiserblumen*. Bryan's speech, which was devoted principally to an attack on the jingo press, was punctuated with shouts of applause (in German, as well as in English), and was given lavish praise in the German-language newspapers on the following morning. A biographer of Bryan has thus described the occasion:

As the former "boy orator of the Platte" banged his fist on the railing of the speaker's platform, his teeth clicked together; his body vibrated; his eyes flashed. Those in the Garden leapt to their feet. They waved American flags. They shouted and they whistled. They stamped their feet and they shrieked. The crowd outside took up the cries and there was a scene of wild commotion.[27]

Henry Weismann to the United German Societies of New York, in the *New-Yorker Staats-Zeitung*, June 23, 1915.

[26] *New-Yorker Staats-Zeitung*, June 18, 20, 24, 1915; *World*, June 25, 1916. See also the *New-Yorker Staats-Zeitung*, June 25, 1915; *New-Yorker Volkszeitung*, June 25, 1915; *Volksblatt und Freiheits-Freund*, June 26, 1915; and *Mitteilungen*, July, 1915, pp. 21–22.

[27] *World*, June 25, 1916; *New Yorker Kampf um Wahrheit und Frieden, aus*

Before the demonstration ended, however, it was to cause Bryan some uneasiness. For in the resolutions which it drew up it reverted to the demand for an arms embargo. It rejected as "unworthy of a great nation" the "specious dictum" (ironically enough, advanced only a few months before by Bryan himself) that "a sovereign state is devoid of the power to alter its laws of export because a foreign war happens to be in progress." "Foisted upon the public by the capitalized money interest," this argument was vitiated by Wilson's embargo on supplies to Mexico. The duty of the United States, the resolutions concluded, was not to any foreign power, but to its own citizens; "the resentment of millions, whose fathers, brothers, and sons are slain by American bullets will naturally and inevitably be far more profound and lasting than the disappointment of those whom we may decline to aid."[28]

There may have been considerable truth in Herman Ridder's assertion that the Madison Square Garden demonstration was "unquestionably the most important protest against war that has ever been made in this country." Yet it hardly settled the differences between the German-Americans and Wilson. Throughout the summer distrust tended to become more and more apparent. At its annual convention in Madison on June 26, the Wisconsin Alliance debated with acerbity a vote of censure against the president. His policy was the object of even more violent attacks when the New York Alliance met at Utica on July 23–25. Weismann caused something of a sensation by denouncing him as "a political bankrupt" and "the dupe of the Wall Street pirates." His third *Lusitania* note, which had been dispatched two days before, was considered as "equivalent to an ultimatum" and "not in accordance with the humanitarian, peace-loving policy of our

den Kriegserinnerungen eines Deutschamerikaners (Ferdinand Hansen), edited by Dr. Franz Rothenfelder (Augsburg, 1917), 37; Genevieve F. and John O. Herrick, *Life of William Jennings Bryan* (Stanton, Chicago, 1925), 302. The occasion seems to have been attended by a surge of crusading fervor, such as Bryan alone could have contributed to any public demonstration.
[28] *World*, June 25, 1915; *Fatherland*, vol. 2, no. 22, pp. 6–7 (July 7, 1915).

Republic." In one resolution passed by the convention it was declared that "we, the German-American Alliance of the State of New York, in convention assembled at Utica, July 23–25, condemn this autocratic action of the President, taken without previous consent of Congress, as a dangerous usurpation of power and a peril to our peace."

Feeling grew even more bitter when, on July 9, the Navy Department took over the Sayville radio station for having emitted messages of a questionable nature. There was particular resentment that the action of the government should follow immediately upon a campaign of exposure against the station in the pro-British *Providence Journal.* In August the bulletin of the Alliance attacked Wilson, along with J. P. Morgan, as the "greatest ally of Great Britain in the United States." This was soon followed by a remarkable report in the *New York Times* to the effect that the Alliance of Elizabeth, New Jersey, had, on August 23, just after the sinking of the *Arabic,* drawn up resolutions indorsing the German submarine campaign and extending to the German naval commanders "the unstinted praise to which they are entitled." A severe condemnation of the government's policy was also issued on the same day by the Ohio Alliance from a meeting which it was holding at Canton.[29]

Between August 2 and August 5 the National Alliance held its eighth convention at San Francisco. This convention, which was the most imposing in the history of the organization, was accompanied by lavish parades and demonstrations and coincided with the 1915 San Francisco exposition. Certain German-language newspapers had already demanded that it define the attitude of the Alliance toward the government

[29] *New Yorker Staats-Zeitung,* June 26, August 24, 1915; *Milwaukee-Sonntagspost,* June 27, 1915; *New York Times,* July 1, 8, 9, 13, 26, 28, August 24, 1915; *World,* July 26, 28, 1915; *Fatherland,* vol. 3, no. 1, p. 12 (August 11, 1915); *Mitteilungen,* August, 1915, pp. 5, 14. On August 28 Ernest Germann, of the Elizabeth Alliance, apologized for the resolutions passed by his branch. It was later denied by some members of the branch that they had even been approved by the meeting of August 23. *New York Times,* August 29, September 9, 1915.

in unmistakable terms, and so a considerable amount of lively discussion was expected.[30]

In his opening address Hexamer dealt critically with the policy of Wilson. On August 4 the convention fell into wild confusion when H. C. Bloedel of Pittsburgh submitted the draft of a letter to the president bitterly denouncing his conduct of public affairs and blaming the United States for the whole diplomatic controversy. "In the eyes of our contemporaries," it was stated, "and before the tribunal of history we stand convicted." Many of the delegates considered the document far too strong, and six officers of the Alliance, including four of its vice-presidents, threatened to resign rather than be responsible for it. In the end Hexamer intervened in favor of moderation.[31]

To the editor of *The Fatherland* this reluctance to employ strong language toward the president was an example of "German-American conservatism."[32] It must be remembered, however, that the aim of the Alliance at this time was not to punish, or even seriously to embarrass, Wilson, but merely to maintain peace.[33] As yet its attitude was not one of vindictiveness. Hence in the resolutions substituted for the Bloedel letter on August 5 the Alliance merely pointed out the mistakes of Wilson's policy and asked for redress:

Since America has declared for neutrality, we demand that our Government adopt a uniform standard in dealing with foreign nations. We deplore that our Government has, in certain ways, allowed England to violate international law and interfere with commerce to the detriment of American interests. It has further allowed in another country—Mexico—the destruction of American life and property, while against Germany it quickly took a threatening and untenable position.[34]

---

[30] *Germania-Herold*, August 2, 3, 1915.
[31] *Ibid.*, August 2, 1915; *World* and *New York Times*, August 5, 1915.
[32] *Fatherland*, vol. 3, no. 2, p. 31 (August 18, 1915).
[33] And, in any case, the attitude of the national organization would naturally tend to be more conservative than that of the branches.
[34] *World*, August 5, 1915; *Germania-Herold*, August 5, 1915.

From the Madison Square Garden demonstration there had emerged a new German-Irish pacifist organization called the Friends of Peace. Its very existence bore testimony to a lack of confidence in Wilson's professed determination to keep the United States out of war. The guiding spirit of the Friends of Peace movement was Henry Weismann, and its mainstay the New York Alliance. The tone of its propaganda was very much that of all other German-American organizations. During July and August it began to spread from New York City to other parts of the country, and to make plans for a national convention in Chicago early in September.[35]

One innovation in policy, however, was to enlist the support of labor. Locally, the unions were attracted by its program of peace. In New York, Homer D. Call, president of the State Federation of Labor, was strongly for it. On August 20 it invited the unions generally to attend its Chicago convention. Here, however, it struck a rock. Samuel Gompers became suspicious and repudiated the whole movement. In a letter to its chairman, John Brisben Walker, on September 2, he branded it as the tool of German militarism, and attacked its promoter, Weismann, with great bitterness. "He has been an active worker in at least half a dozen different movements, each the very antithesis of the others, and in no movement with which he has been connected has he proved himself other than an apostate." Gompers also charged that "paid emissaries" of the movement had been sent out to buy over some of the labor leaders. The letter, much to Weismann's embarrassment, was given wide publicity by the press.[36]

The convention, which to the imaginative editor of the *Illinois Staats-Zeitung* would make Chicago "a new Jerusa-

[35] By the end of August, 1915, the following organizations had affiliated with the Friends of Peace: the German-American Alliance, the Roman Catholic Central Verein, the American Independence Union, the Labor Peace League, the League of Irish-American Associations, and the Star Spangled Banner Association. *Milwaukee-Sonntagspost*, August 29, 1915.

[36] *New-Yorker Staats-Zeitung*, August 15, September 4, 1915; Singer's *Jahrbuch*, 1916, pp. 229, 230; *New York Times*, September 3, 4, 1915; *Illinois Staats-Zeitung*, September 4, 1915.

lem," was to be a rally of all who distrusted the policy
of President Wilson. It was to be no local affair, Weismann
declared, "but a demonstration of millions of peace-loving
citizens of the whole country." Its immediate purpose, as defined in an appeal issued by John Brisben Walker, was "to
protest against America's entry into the war." Further, it
would discuss the question of appointing delegations to visit
the belligerent countries in the hope of bringing about peace,
and also urge a special session of Congress "to reconsider the
advisability of placing an embargo on all war supplies." In
addition to Bryan, it was proposed to have on the platform
Charles W. Fairbanks, Charles Nagel, Jane Addams, Mayor
William Hale Thompson, Governor Edward F. Dunne, Senators La Follette, Hoke Smith, Works, Hitchcock, and Clapp,
and Congressmen Mann, Buchanan, and Porter.[37]

It must have been a relief to the supporters of the administration when the convention ended in something of a fiasco.
It met on September 4–5, and Weismann's delegation of four
hundred, which he gathered from the Alliances of New York
and New Jersey, showed where its main strength lay.[38] It was,
in fact, little more than a German-American affair. With the
exception of Bryan, its speakers—Weismann, Vollmer,
Koelble, Dr. Berkemeier, and O'Leary—had criticized Wilson
at scores of meetings held by the Alliance. On September 6 it
was greeted with headlines of ridicule in the Chicago newspapers, after its delegates had received with mingled hissing
and applause the news of the sinking of the *Hesperian*. Bryan
himself was visibly embarrassed when it proceeded to draw
up resolutions for freedom of commerce in non-contraband

[37] *Illinois Staats-Zeitung*, September 4, 1915; *Milwaukee-Sonntagspost*, August
1, 29, 1915; *Fatherland*, vol. 2, no. 26, p. 4 (August 4, 1915); *New-Yorker Staats-
Zeitung*, August 22, 1915. Many of the persons named declined to attend the
meeting.
[38] *Illinois Staats-Zeitung*, September 5, 1915. "Die Deutschamerikaner überwiegen an Zahl jeden anderen Teil unserer Bevölkerung fremden Blutes und
deshalb überwiegen sie auch in dieser Konvention." *Volksblatt und Freiheits-
Freund*, September 5, 1915.

HENRY WEISMANN
President of the New York State Alliance

goods, an embargo on munitions, and a refusal of loans to belligerents, in which he found it impossible to concur.[39]

With Wilson's approval of the Reading-Blackett mission, the German-Americans became all the more convinced of his unneutrality. The German-language press printed one attack after another in its editorial columns; some newspapers, like the *Illinois Staats-Zeitung,* voiced their indignation in English as well as in German. Severe condemnation greeted his reply of August 13 to the Austro-Hungarian protest against the munitions trade, when the Jackson Alliance of Michigan held its annual convention on September 5. His note to Vienna, it was asserted, showed that his policy would follow the usual course of hypocrisy and the dictates of Wall Street rather than the wishes of the American people.[40] Whatever Germany did, it was lamented at the convention of the Oklahoma Alliance on September 13, was condemned beforehand: "England is treated with kid gloves, while Germany is handled with a club."[41]

Leaders of the Alliance began to deal less and less kindly with the president. Hexamer, it will be recalled, had exerted a "conservative" influence at the eighth convention of the National Alliance at San Francisco. On November 22, however, during a propaganda tour of Wisconsin, he declared at Milwaukee that "we have never had such a pitiful, weak-kneed administration as at present." At the same time Alphonse G. Koelble, of the United German Societies of New York, published in leaflet form an "Open Letter" to the president, in which he stated that "the last American note to England is irrefutable corroboration of the flagrancy, the number, and the gravity of the British invasions of American rights, and your administration's total failure to stop them; and

[39] *New Yorker Kampf um Wahrheit und Frieden,* 60–81; *New York Times,* September 6, 7, 1915; *New-Yorker Staats-Zeitung,* September 7, 1915; *Germania-Herold,* September 7, 1915; Singer's *Jahrbuch,* 1916, p. 249.

[40] This was the United States government's reply to the Austro-Hungarian note of June 14, 1915. See the *New York Times,* August 14, 1915.

[41] *Mitteilungen,* October, 1915, p. 35.

your demand to do so is, in its weakness, in striking contrast to your 'ultimata' to Germany."[42]

Thus by the end of 1915 German-American attempts to keep the United States to a course of strict neutrality and of peace with Germany had developed into a campaign against Wilson personally. For several months there had been hints that he might not prove a *persona grata* in the election of 1916, and if we may believe a letter of Henry Cabot Lodge to Roosevelt, written on September 25, some of the Democratic Party leaders were becoming a little afraid of the "German agitation." As early as May, 1915, the bulletin of the Alliance had pronounced it "a piece of capital folly" to entrust Wilson again with the destinies of the nation: "the handwriting on the wall should be made perfectly legible for Mr. Wilson." As a matter of fact, it had become more and more legible. On May 28 the St. Louis Alliance had threatened to stop at nothing, within the rights of citizenship, to change the neutrality of the government. At the celebration of German Day by the German-American Societies of the District of Columbia on October 19, one speaker hailed the German vote as the instrument of Wilson's doom. On October 25 the Massachusetts Alliance took a firm stand against his re-election, amid cries of "alienism" from the *New York Times*. And when, on November 18, the drive against him was joined by the Friends of Peace, the *New-Yorker Staats-Zeitung* expressed its satisfaction in no uncertain terms. "The die is cast," it rejoiced. "The first step in the campaign against renomination has been taken."[43]

[42] *Germania-Herold,* November 23, 1915; *An Open Letter to the President of the United States, by an American Citizen* (written by Alphonse G. Koelble and published by him in New York, November, 1915), leaflet F83614.KO in the library of the State Historical Society of Wisconsin.

[43] *Selections from the Correspondence of Theodore Roosevelt and Henry Cabot Lodge, 1884–1918* (Scribners, New York, 1925), 2:463; *Mitteilungen,* May, 1915, p. 4; November, 1915, p. 9; *Westliche Post* (St. Louis), May 29, 1915; *Illinois Staats-Zeitung,* October 20, 1915; *New-Yorker Staats-Zeitung,* October 25, November 19, 1915; *New York Times,* October 26, 1915.

V

"SWATTING THE HYPHEN"[1]

WHILE THE GERMAN-AMERICANS WERE DOING THEIR BEST TO discredit Wilson, attempts were being made to discredit them. During the campaign of 1916 the country was to hear much about the "hyphen"—a somewhat uninspiring piece of grammatical terminology which came to have for a time a remarkable political significance. Applied almost exclusively to the German-Americans, it was used to suggest a sort of hiatus in their loyalty to the United States. It gave the impression that they were still Germans as much as Americans, and that they would stand by Germany even though America suffered. Whether, like many other scare-raising, vote-winning catchwords of politics, it ever contained even a germ of truth it would not be easy to establish.[2]

Loyalty is always a difficult matter to assess. At times in American history, as during the Revolution, when in a way it marked the line of division between the two opposing forces, it has been a really fundamental issue. In the form, however, in which it was dressed up by the press and the public speaker in 1915 and 1916, it is hard to treat it with any such seriousness. An ingenious product of anti-German propaganda, it became a convenient political shibboleth for those who feared the German-American vote in the election of 1916. There never was any real danger that the German-American leaders would prove disloyal to the United States. Some of them had been born here. Many of them had come

[1] This title is suggested by the *Literary Digest*, 51:943–944 (October 30, 1915), which characterized the attacks upon certain groups of German-Americans as a "Swat-the-Hyphen" movement.

[2] See Horace L. Brand, "Der Bindestrich," in Singer's *Jahrbuch*, 1917, pp. 229–233. The *World* (New York), (November 10, 1915) referred to the question, somewhat picturesquely, as "The New Copperheadism."

here not to serve the cause of Germany but to take advantage
of opportunities for material advancement that had been lack-
ing in Germany. Socially they belonged for the most part to
the well-to-do middle class, with their economic roots more
firmly implanted in the American system than many of those
who raised the charge of disloyalty against them. They had
everything to lose by not being American first—and were
frank enough to admit it.

Their organization, the German-American Alliance, had
admittedly been pro-German after 1914. But this did not
make it the instrument of the German Foreign Office any
more than the fervent pro-Ally sympathies of many other
Americans made them subjects of Britain or France. It had
used violent language in its criticisms of the president—but
not so violent as that of Colonel Roosevelt, one of their most
bitter and persistent accusers. It had striven for peace and
neutrality in 1915, but it could also present evidence that this
was primarily in the interests of the United States and not of
Germany.

To the historian the whole "hyphen-loyalty" issue is a significant reflection of the extent to which the European war
projected itself into and dominated the election campaign of
1916. It indicates the extent to which Americans had already
digested the arguments of the Allied propagandists, for these
had been frequently directed against the Germans in the
United States. As we shall see, much of the campaign of
vituperation was of avowedly British origin.[3] For propaganda
purposes the German-Americans were invariably treated as

---

[3] Although not necessarily the product of any propaganda agency connected
with the British government. Much of the British propaganda was written
by American citizens. It took the form of articles published in British maga-
zines or books published by British publishers. There is no reason to
believe—as the German-language press at times asserted—that these writers
were subsidized. They were persons of high integrity, who believed, in all
sincerity, in the justice of the Allied cause. It lies indeed in the very nature
of men to take sides in such a crisis, without any prospect of pecuniary gain;
in fact they are generally willing to suffer losses to see their side win.

Professor W. Macneile Dixon, one of the directors of the British Department
of Information during the war, denies that this agency made any attempt to

Germans in America rather than as American citizens. Whatever they attempted as an organized body in public affairs
was assumed to have a specifically German motive. "The pro-
British propaganda," wrote Max Heinrici of the press bureau
of the Alliance, in April, 1916, "has of late devoted its especial
attention to the National German-American Alliance. Whenever there has been, through some form of perversion or
other, an opportunity to cast suspicion upon the activity of
the Alliance, and to ascribe to it aims that are disloyal and
unpatriotic, it has been used with all intensity."[4]

It was in this connection that fertile imaginations began
to see in the Alliance an agent of Pan-Germanism. For the
first fifteen years of its existence no one had questioned its
right to be considered a truly American institution, but now,
upon looking back over its history, a few ingenious opponents
suddenly found cause to suspect it of being the child of pre-
war German policy. Even Bryan, as we have seen, in endeavoring to pay court to the German-Americans in his appeal of
June 11, 1915, assumed that they had some sort of influence
with the German government.

Cartoonist and columnist united in a campaign against the
hyphen all through the later months of 1915. At this time
there were almost daily exposures of German and Austro-

influence the course of American domestic politics: "The Department of
Information . . . never made the slightest attempt to interfere in American
politics, if for no other reason than that no one in the Department had the
knowledge of its complexities, its currents, and counter-currents which would
have made such intrusion or interference in any manner or degree effective
or even possible. Nor had we money for such operations. . . . There were
of course thousands of articles, books, pamphlets written by private partizans
of both sides, both in the United States and other countries, with which
we in our Department had nothing whatever to do, though no doubt they
were frequently ascribed to us or our agents. . . . We in the Department of
Information . . . were quite incapable of any effort to discredit the German-
American vote, and in point of fact never made any effort to do so." Letter to
the writer, March 4, 1938. We have no reason to doubt this statement. Yet
the fact remains that many "unofficial" British propagandists and free-lances
were keenly interested in the American domestic situation. Some of them
undoubtedly saw in the hyphen-baiting campaign and the pre-election struggle
of 1916 an opportunity to prostrate the German-Americans as a political force
in the United States.

[4] *Germania-Herold* (Milwaukee), April 20, 1916.

Hungarian conspiracies in the United States, the *Providence Journal* making them its specialty. Today these conspiracies fill five pages of the *New York Times Index* for the months of October to December. Although the persons concerned were all German subjects, it was not difficult to embarrass the German-Americans by suggesting some remote form of collusion on their part. Thus the New York *World,* in an exposure of German propaganda which it began on August 15, 1915, proved that there had been cooperation between the German Dr. Albert and the German-American George Sylvester Viereck. At the same time it discovered that Henry Weismann had a record—political rather than criminal, it omitted to explain—with the police of San Francisco.[5] The *Literary Digest,* not as a rule unkindly disposed toward the German-Americans, had, in dealing with the Washington conference on February 13, printed a photograph of Richard Bartholdt between pictures of Van Horn and the Vanceboro Bridge which he had attempted to blow up. The Philadelphia *Public Record* suggested in October that the drive against the Allied loan was akin to the acts of sabotage in the munitions factories. To these allegations was added, early in 1916, the rumor that among Von Igel's papers had been found the names of ten thousand German-Americans who had pledged themselves to Germany in the event of a war with the United States.[6]

Theodore Roosevelt and the New York Democratic press found themselves in unusual agreement on the hyphen question. It had not taken long for the colonel's anti-German sentiments after 1914 to cool off his old friendship for the German-Americans. In the first year of the war he developed an attitude of bitter antipathy. On October 12, in an address to

[5] In 1886 he had been sentenced to six months imprisonment in connection with the anti-Chinese agitation. He was then a member of the Socialist Labor Party. *World,* August 1, 1915.

[6] *Literary Digest,* 50:301 (February 13, 1915); 51:944 (October 30, 1915, quoting from the *Public Record*); *Times,* May 5, 1916.

the Knights of Columbus in New York, he launched the first of
many attacks. There was no room proper in this country for
the hyphenated American, he declared, for one could not
hoist two flags on the same pole and not have one underneath
the other. Five days later, and possibly upon this inspiration,
the *New York Times* joined in the campaign. In an editorial
devoted to the "Standard-Bearers of the Hyphen" it scoffingly
suggested Bryan as a candidate for president in 1916 with the
slogan "the dove against the vulture." For vice-president it
offered Charles John Hexamer, on a program of "anything
to injure the United States."[7]

Wilson himself professed to regard the hyphen question
with all seriousness. He had thought with solicitude, he
wrote to House on August 25, 1915, of a possible outbreak of
German-Americans in the United States in the event of a war
with Germany, but he was in doubt as to where and how the
government should prepare. Every clue had been followed up,
even the most vague, but nothing had been discovered sufficient to form a basis even for guessing. House, too, seemed a
little perturbed, and in his reply discussed specifically what
the nature of the outbreak might be. He on his part did not
look for "any organized rebellion or outbreak, but merely
some degree of frightfulness in order to intimidate the country."[8]

The president soon began to express his misgivings publicly. On October 11, in an address to the Daughters of the
American Revolution in Washington, he declared himself
"in a hurry for an opportunity to have a line up" between the
loyal and disloyal citizens. On November 4, in outlining be-

[7] *World,* October 13, 1915; *Times,* October 17, 1915. In the years before the
war Roosevelt had been extremely popular among the German-Americans, and
had been elected to honorary membership of many of their clubs. On October
5, 1908, he had, as president of the United States, sent Hexamer his "heartiest
good wishes for the success of the National German-American Alliance on the
occasion of its gathering to celebrate the 225th anniversary of the first German
emigration to this country." Von Bosse, *Ein Kampf um Glauben und Volkstum,*
190.
[8] Seymour, *Intimate Papers of Colonel House,* 2:33–35.

fore the Manhattan Club the government's plans for preparedness, he dealt with the hyphen question at some length.
With the Alliance and its subsidiaries doubtless in mind, he
referred to "small groups whom it is high time the Nation
should call to a reckoning." The government was feeling
grave concern, he added, that "voices have been raised in
America professing to be the voices of Americans, which were
not indeed and in truth American, but which spoke alien
sympathies. . . . These voices have not been many, but they
have been loud and very clamorous. They have proceeded
from a few who were bitter and who were grievously mislead."
By December 7 he had become so agitated by the question
that he introduced it into his third annual address to Congress:

There are citizens of the United States, I blush to admit, born
under other flags but welcomed under our generous naturalization
laws to the full freedom and opportunity of America, who have
poured the poison of disloyalty into the very arteries of our
national life; who have sought to bring the authority and good
name of our government into contempt, to destroy our industries
wherever they thought it effective for their vindictive purpose to
strike at them, and to debase our policies to the uses of foreign
intrigue. . . .[9]

With the president of the United States thus publicly ques-
tioning the loyalty of some German-Americans it was not difficult for the press and the professional propagandists to make
people accept their insinuations. Chief of the hyphen-baiters
was the *World,* which concentrated obdurately upon the
German-American Alliance throughout 1916. On March 7
it came out with the following headlines, spread in large type
across its front page:

[9] *The Public Papers of Woodrow Wilson: The New Democracy,* edited by
Ray S. Baker and William E. Dodd (Harper, New York, 1926), 1:379, 390–391,
424–425; *Times,* October 12, November 5, December 8, 1915. "Ein Dokument,"
commented the *New-Yorker Staats-Zeitung* (December 8, 1915) on the address
of December 7, "würdeloser als dieses, steht in den Annalen der amerikanischen
Geschichte nicht verzeichnet."

GERMAN LOBBY, IN "AMERICAN" DISGUISE, SPURS THE CONGRESS FIGHT
ON WILSON; PLOTS TO CONTROL NATIONAL CONVENTION

Direct Propaganda, Abandoned after World's Exposures Reappears in Secret Organizations backed by German-American Alliance—Lobbyist Reports on his Efforts with Leaders in Fight on President—Worked with Gore and Stephens to Blend their Bills and Says they asked Aid of his Society for Propaganda in Armed Ships Fight.

The occasion was the debate on the Gore and McLemore resolutions to prevent Americans from traveling upon armed merchant ships of belligerents. These resolutions, according to the *World,* were the work of the Alliance: "documentary evidence in the possession of the *World* shows that the driving force back of the Gore Resolution and the McLemore Resolution is the National German-American Alliance." For its congressional campaign the Alliance was charged with maintaining a "clearing house" in New York under the direction of Alphonse G. Koelble. The objects of the campaign were as follows:

1. Refusal of passports to Americans travelling on the ships of belligerents.

2. An embargo on contraband of war.

3. The prohibiting of Federal Banks from subscribing to foreign loans.

This is the immediate work. Back of it is a comprehensive program for the control of the Republican National Convention and the defeat of President Wilson in the interest of the German cause. This plan is known to the inside coterie of German leaders who are in charge of the work as the "Wisconsin Idea," because it was formally indorsed by the *Wisconsin Staatsverband des Deutschamerikanischen Nationalbundes* [Wisconsin State Alliance]. The idea itself, however, originated with Dr. Hexamer, President of the German-American Alliance.[10]

Around these charges the *World* wove a sordid story of conspiracy and intrigue. By means honest or otherwise someone

[10] *World,* March 7, 1916.

had procured for it an assortment of rather confidential documents from the office of Alphonse G. Koelble, president of
the United German Societies of New York. These it reproduced in its edition of March 7. One was a circular sent
out by Henry Weismann in December, 1915. To anyone who
had hitherto heard little of the Alliance and was unfamiliar
with the nature of its appeals, this had at least the flavor of
sensation, if not of suspicion. The next document was a "confidential circular," alleged to have been issued after a visit
of Koelble to Germany in the summer of 1915, "providing
for the secret but complete organization of German-Americans
as a unit in politics." (There were several millions of them,
and exactly how such numbers could have been organized
in complete secrecy the *World* failed to explain.) Koelble's
so-called German lobby was declared to be one of the results
of this circular.

The rest of the exposé consisted of facsimiles and reprints
of Koelble's correspondence. There were three letters written
to him by a certain J. T. Marsalis, who, according to the
World, was the chief lobbyist of the Alliance in Washington.
Marsalis had obviously been in the capital during all the debates on the Gore and McLemore resolutions, and had held
conversations with their sponsors. These three letters were
really the most suggestive evidence that the *World* produced.
There was also a letter of January 13, 1916, from Hexamer
to Koelble, urging him to support the resolutions; an undated
letter from Leo Stern to Koelble, discussing the Wisconsin
Idea; two letters, of December 21 and December 28, 1915,
from Bartholdt to Koelble, also discussing the Wisconsin
Idea and suggesting a Champ Clark boom in New York; and
a letter of December 22, 1915, from Weismann to Koelble,
strongly opposing the Idea.

The *World* exposé was one of the great sensations of that
altogether sensational session of Congress. It produced unmistakable consternation and confusion among those many

congressmen and senators who found themselves named, not always correctly, as having had dealings with the Alliance. Not the least embarrassed, of course, was Gore himself, whose resolution had been defeated on March 3 after a certain amount of pressure had been exerted by the president. A vote on the McLemore resolution was taken at 6:43 P.M. on March 7, when the *World* exposé had already been published. It was defeated by 276 votes to 142.[11]

Officials at the White House and the Department of State, it was reported, were of the opinion that the exposé was "one of much importance." The president was said to have been convinced that it indicated a widespread pro-German plot. In the view of his secretary, Joseph Tumulty, writing some years afterward, the Gore resolution was the outcome of "a sinister purpose on the part of German sympathizers in this country to give Germany full sway upon the high seas, in order that she might be permitted to carry on her unlawful and inhuman submarine warfare." [12]

A few newspaper editors, reading the *World* of March 7 a little more critically than had obviously been expected, refused to see evidence of a German conspiracy. But many pointed to the Alliance as the sponsor of the Gore and McLemore resolutions. The editor of the *Times,* who soon had a little quarrel of his own with the Alliance for "bullying" eleven of the congressmen from Minnesota, was particularly impressed. In his opinion the documents published by the *World* were "an astounding chapter in the continued story of German conspiracy against the United States." They were proof, he added, that the Alliance had organized a campaign to promote legislation favorable to the designs and interests of Germany.[13]

---

[11] See the *World,* March 8, 1916.

[12] *Ibid.,* March 8, 1916; *Literary Digest,* 52:699 (March 18, 1916); Joseph P. Tumulty, *Woodrow Wilson as I Know Him* (Literary Digest Edition, 1921), 202.

[13] *Literary Digest,* 52:699 (March 18, 1916); editorial comments reprinted in the *World,* March 9, 1916; *Times,* March 8, 22, 1916.

Ever since the Gore and McLemore resolutions had come before Congress the *World* had attacked them as pro-German measures. In one fiery editorial after another Frank Cobb had weighed the whole issue as a struggle between the kaiser and the president for the control of the United States government. Rollin Kirby had lent his inimitable talent as a cartoonist to portray the German ruler, in his characteristic pose, dominating the halls of the American Capitol. Hence when the accusing finger was pointed to the Alliance, as the means by which the kaiser sought to exert his influence in Washington, the charge was doubly crushing; to be named as the culprit after two months sustained talk of treason tended to place the organization in a particularly unenviable situation. Against so tremendous an opponent as the *World* it was, in any case, at a considerable disadvantage in defending itself, at least before the English-speaking public.

While we may be grateful to the *World* for having made available for historical purposes a few private German-American letters which might otherwise have been destroyed (and yet the authenticity of which was admitted even by Koelble himself),[14] it is impossible to accept in all seriousness the interpretation which it placed upon them. It was a simple story: a few burgled papers, some of them marked confidential, their true meaning a mystery because of their incompleteness and lack of arrangement; therefore to the fertile imagination of the newspaper man they presented the unmistakable clues to a vast conspiracy. Yet perhaps the only really sinister attribute of the documents was the means by which they had come into the possession of the *World*.

The letter from Weismann to Koelble of December, 1915, was actually an appeal from the New York State Alliance for

---

[14] "No denial was made yesterday of the authenticity of any of the letters or documents reproduced in the *World*. Alphonse G. Koelble admitted that his letters were published in the *World* as he had written or received them. Weismann admitted that the *World* printed an accurate copy of his letter to Koelble." *World*, March 8, 1916.

some form of protest against Wilson's address to Congress of December 7, and for renewed efforts for German war relief work.[15] It was published openly in *Mitteilungen* for January, 1916. Hexamer's letter to Koelble was one of many sent to local Alliance leaders in support of the Gore resolution. It was published in the German-language press on January 30.[16] Had the Alliance been contemplating the establishment of a "secret organization" to control American politics in the interest of Germany, it seems hardly likely that it would have made its plans so public. Had the editor of the *World* perchance also read the bulletin of the Alliance for January, 1916, or any leading German-language newspaper of January 30, it is doubtful whether he would have seen much honest use in publishing these documents in his exposé of March 7.

No leader of the Alliance would have denied, of course, that he was heartily in favor of the Gore and McLemore resolutions. For these would have removed the submarine question from the immediate attention of the United States government and thereby have ended the main source of friction between this country and Germany. The Alliance could argue that by supporting the resolutions it was saving the United States rather than helping Germany. In his appeal of June 11, 1915, Bryan had suggested such a measure to the German-Americans[17] and now it was being sponsored by more than one representative of the nation in Congress. It was therefore hard, without having recourse to the peculiar logic of certain government supporters, to appreciate why to work for the resolutions was entirely un-American.

It is significant that the Alliance was as strongly for the principle of the Gore and McLemore resolutions after the *World* exposé as before. In April, 1916, John B. Mayer of the Central Alliance of Pennsylvania even attempted to in-

[15] *Mitteilungen*, January, 1916, p. 20.
[16] See, for example, the *Milwaukee-Sonntagspost*, January 30, 1916, and the *New-Yorker Staats-Zeitung*, April 3, 1916.
[17] *World*, June 12, 1915.

duce his congressman to introduce another such measure. It is doubtful whether the Alliance would have returned so suddenly to this course of alleged delinquency had it really felt itself exposed and whipped as a conspirator by the *World*.[18]

On behalf of the Alliance, Hexamer denied all idea of a lobby. Koelble, who insisted that the documents had been obtained by burglary, said that Marsalis was neither representing him nor any organization with which he was connected. The bulletin of the Alliance for April, 1916, chose to ignore the documents which the *World* had published, but defended at considerable length the right to support the Gore and McLemore resolutions: "The agitation of the German-Americans in favor of the resolutions," it said, "was justified and in every respect within the bounds of their rights as citizens of the United States. . . . The National Alliance and other organizations may still continue their agitation in favor of measures with which they are in sympathy. They have a right to do so and no one can prevent them."[19]

Perhaps the most direct attack upon the Alliance before the United States entered the war, this exposé was but the outstanding one of many incidents in the campaign against the hyphen. Fully aware that no reply from the Alliance could ever reach the same wide circle of readers as his own newspaper, the editor of the *World* continued to press his charges with a frequent indifference to the true facts. Throughout the months preceding the election his reporters scrutinized its every movement, knowing all the time exactly what it was doing—and sometimes more.

On March 19, 1916, the *World* came out with the peremptory demand that the Alliance be disbanded. Since August, 1914, it argued, its loyalty to "the Kaiser, to the

[18] *New-Yorker Staats-Zeitung*, April 27, 1916; *Mitteilungen*, April, 1916, pp. 2–3, 19.
[19] *Ibid.*, April, 1916, pp. 1–2; *World*, March 7, 1916.

Hohenzollerns, and to Prussian autocracy" had never wavered:

Whenever American rights have conflicted with German military necessity the National German-American Alliance has been staunchly on the side of Germany.

That Alliance is now waging a bitter political warfare upon the President of the United States because he refused to make the United States an ally of the Teutonic Powers. It is plotting to gain control of the Republican National Convention in order to Prussianize the foreign policies of the United States. . . .

No other country in the world would tolerate such an organization under a national charter. Why should the United States tolerate it?[20]

On April 23, under the headlines "Germans Organize to Control Elections in the United States," the *World* published another exposé as "proof of a campaign, with headquarters here, to throw the hyphenated vote only to senatorial and other candidates more loyal to Germany than their own country." Again the unhappy Koelble, who seems to have had an unfailing knack of allowing his most private correspondence to fall into the hands of his enemies, became the object of suspicion. Allegations centered around a letter of March 24 addressed to Koelble from Oscar B. Colquitt, former governor of Texas and now a candidate for the United States Senate. In the letter Colquitt attempted to solicit German-American support. From it the *World* deduced that "central campaign headquarters to control United States elections in the interest of Germany have been established in New York City." The directors of these headquarters were Bernard Ridder of the *New-Yorker Staats-Zeitung*, Alphonse G. Koelble, and Henry Weismann.[21] Inspired by this remarkable discovery, the *World* also authorized inquiries in Texas, as

[20] *World*, March 19, 1916.
[21] The *World* blundered badly in mentioning Weismann in this connection, for he was, at the time, trying to keep the Alliance out of the election. See below, page 120.

a result of which it claimed to have found twenty counties "absolutely controlled by the German vote." [22]

The attacks of the *World* on the Alliance bore a striking resemblance to those of the British propagandists. The latter had made an early entry into the field with their campaign against the German-Americans. On April 17, 1915, there appeared in the *Living Age* a reprint from the British *National Review* of an anonymous article on "The Germanization of the United States." This charged that a propaganda *Bund* had been organized by the German embassy in Washington, and that the Alliance had promised its full support. Plans were also being made to exert "great pressure" in American politics "through the medium of the German vote." [23] On May 29 there followed an article by Annie E. Lane on "The German-American," which was reprinted from the *Nineteenth Century*. This warned of the "Berlin threats of reprisals" against American policy "through the German-Americans at the polls." The German-Americans were described as a sort of political club with which the German government would wreak its vengeance upon the Wilson administration. "When one opens certain pro-German papers published in America one has a sense of being deafened by the uncontrolled fury of their propaganda. America is threatened unless she is properly neutral, and properly neutral, according to Germany, means to favor Germany." [24]

A third article, which the *Living Age* reprinted on June 26 from the British *New Statesman,* sounded even graver misgivings. This, which bore the title of "Germany and German-America," pointed an accusing finger at the American Neutrality League. The league, which, as we have seen, was merely

---

[22] *World,* April 23, 24, 1916.
[23] *Living Age,* 285:131–137 (April 17, 1915). "British influence in this country, on the other hand," naïvely remarked the writer, "is of small practical importance." This scarcely flattered J. P. Morgan and Company.
[24] *Ibid.,* 285:520–526 (May 29, 1915). Annie E. Lane, American-born novelist, was the wife of the London publisher John Lane.

an Irish-American extension of the local Alliances, was pronounced more "dangerous" than Bernstorff, Dernburg, the Ridders, Viereck, or any other of the German propagandists, although it omitted to explain how even these were "dangerous"—so far as the United States was concerned. Then it reverted to the question of "the organized German vote," and concluded: "In states like Illinois and Wisconsin, or cities like Chicago and Milwaukee, the political vote must of necessity be complicated by the racial issue. That is understood. But it becomes another matter when candidates are run as Germans, and votes are sought for them on the ground that their election would count towards the salvation of the Fatherland."[25]

In the summer of 1915 there appeared in the United States a small book published in London under the title *The German-American Plot*. It was written by Frederic William Wile, who before the war had been shared as correspondent in Berlin by the London *Daily Mail* and the *Chicago Tribune*.[26] Since then he had made a tour of the United States to investigate the activities of the German-Americans, during which he had interviewed Hexamer (whom he charged with being Dernburg's assistant as propagandist for the German government) and other leaders of the Alliance. To Wile the whole German-American movement was a "plot." He even dealt with the Washington conference of January 30, 1915, in a chapter on "Terrorization." From the conference he traced the rise of a "German Party" which would sway American politics in the interests of Berlin:

The "German vote" is the best organized "foreign vote" in the country. It has always been considered the only one which can be "delivered" *en bloc* to party managers, thanks to its compact organization. . . . That Kaiserism expects to wield the balance of power in American politics during the next two years is amply

[25] *Ibid.*, 285:818–821 (June 26, 1915).
[26] See the *Germania-Herold*, September 8, 1914.

evident from the remarkable resolutions adopted by the new
German Party at its constituent assembly in Washington on January 30. . . .

Throughout the entire book the German-Americans were
branded as disloyal, those of the Middle West being the particular object of attack. "If Milwaukee may be considered as
a criterion, German-Americans are German first, and Americans afterwards, if at all."[27]

The palpable absurdity of Wile's charges did not prevent
his book from gaining a very favorable reception. One of the
many who reviewed it with lavish praise was Sidney Brooks,
who devoted an entire article to it in the *Outlook*. Wile, he
declared (not without a touch of flattery, as it now appears),
had "a good eye for the realities of a situation." The United
States had "not yet heard the last of the German-American
plot." Statistically a strong case might easily be made out "to
convince the Wilhelmstrasse that it was in its power, with
very little dexterity, to manipulate American opinion and
policy pretty much as it chose."[28]

In October, 1915, there was published in London for
American consumption another book on *German Conspiracies in America,* written, according to its title-page, "from an
American point of view, by an American." Its author was
one William H. Skaggs. Like the other attacks upon the German-Americans which proceeded from Allied sources, this
book emphasized their readiness to enter politics. One of its
chapters was headed "Meddling in American Politics," another "Kaiserism or Constitution." The climax of "German
impudence and bumptiousness," it was declared, "came when
German-American Leagues [i.e., Alliances] undertook to dic-

---

[27] Frederic W. Wile, *The German-American Plot* (Pearson, London, 1915),
14, 116. The book had originally appeared in the *Daily Mail* (London), in the
spring of 1915.
[28] The article is reprinted in the *Living Age*, 286:440–443 (August 14, 1915).
For a German-American review of Wile's book see the editorial in the
Germania-Herold, August 2, 1915.

tate candidates, control political conventions and primaries, and by a system of boycotting and bluffing, intrigue and corrupt practices, German propagandism has undertaken to control the election of national, state, and municipal officials."[29]

Not even the *New York Times* was impervious to some of the outstanding revelations of German-American intrigue made by the British propagandists. On March 12, 1916, it printed a remarkable story from William Le Queux's *German Spies in England,* the object of which was to convey the impression that the German-American Alliance used its influence in American politics in the interests of German policy, and that its national president, Dr. Hexamer, was a sort of imperial viceroy. The story, which an investigation commissioned for the present writer by the former kaiser Wilhelm II himself has proved to be as fictitious as some of the better literature that Le Queux wrote, concerned an alleged secret council meeting held at Potsdam in June, 1908, a report of which was said to have found its way into British archives through "a German official of high position, who holds pro-British views."[30] According to Le Queux, the kaiser told the meeting that it lay in Germany's immediate power to conquer the world. As it was, the German-Americans had brought America under German hegemony:

Even now I rule supreme in the United States, where almost one half of the population is either of German birth or of German descent, and where 3,000,000 voters do my bidding at the Presidential elections. No American administration could remain in power against the will of the German voters, who through that admirable organization, the German-American National League

[29] William H. Skaggs, *German Conspiracies in America* (Fisher Unwin, London, 1915), 189. French as well as British propagandists accused the German-Americans of going into politics in the interests of Germany. See Louis Rouquette, *La Propagande germanique aux États-Unis* (Chapelot, Paris, 1916). "Faut-il aussi mentionner le nouveau parti politique qu'ils viennent d'organiser et qui a pour but de punir aux prochaines élections ceux qui se sont permis de critiquer l'Allemagne ou qui ont refusé de se prêter aux machinations du député Bartholdt?" Page 29.
[30] That is, a spy.

[i.e., Alliance] of the United States of America, control the destinies of the vast republic beyond the sea. If a man was ever worthy of a high decoration at my hands it was Herr Dr. Hexamer, the President of the League, who may justly be termed to be, by my grace, the acting ruler of all the Germans in the United States.[31]

One of the most bitter and persistent opponents of the German-American cause was Gustavus Ohlinger, president of the Toledo Chamber of Commerce and a writer of some ability. It was he, as much as anyone, who popularized the idea that the Alliance was a branch of Pan-Germanism. Ohlinger's first attack came in April, 1916, when he published in the *Atlantic Monthly* an article on "German Propaganda in the United States." In this he traced the activities of the German-Americans since the beginning of the war and denounced "those Germans who are only geographically and politically Americans." In his treatment of the Alliance he was particularly virulent, charging that it had pursued "a

[31] *New York Times,* March 12, 1916. On February 5, 1938, the writer sent a copy of Le Queux's story to the former kaiser Wilhelm II at Doorn Castle, Holland, to obtain the latter's comments. Apparently the letter was passed on to the Generalverwaltung des vormaligen Preussischen Königshauses in Berlin, with the injunction to investigate the matter. The investigation showed that the meeting of which Le Queux spoke never even took place. The writer received from the Generalverwaltung the following reply, dated March 24, 1938: "Sehr geehrter Herr Child! Seine Majestät Kaiser Wilhelm II, hat mich mit der Beantwortung Ihres Schreibens vom 5. Februar d. Js. beauftragt. Sie bitten um eine Antwort auf die Frage, ob Seine Majestät in einer geheimen Beratung—secret council meeting—die in Potsdam im Jahre 1908 abgehalten worden sein soll, eine Rede gehalten hat, aus der Sie den nachstehenden Passus wörtlich wiedergeben: [*here follows a report of the speech quoted above*]. Auf Grund der angestellten Nachforschungen hat eine solche geheime Beratung überhaupt nicht stattgefunden. Die oben angegebenen Worte sind, wie Sie selbst annehmen, niemals von Seiner Majestät gesprochen worden. Ich bin Ihnen sehr dankbar dafür, dass Sie mir Gelegenheit gegeben haben, diese Verleumdung Seiner Majestät klarzustellen und darf Sie darum bitten, diese Klarstellung in entsprechender Weise zu verwerten. Mit vorzüglicher Hochachtung, [*signed*] Von Dommes."

There is also every reason, from the very nature of the document itself, to condemn it as a forgery. Earlier in the speech the kaiser is said to have boasted that he would "make, once and for all, good the words of our poet: 'Deutschland über Alles.' Yes, gentlemen, Germany over everything in the world, the first power on earth, both in peace and war." Now to a German-speaking person (and surely the kaiser was such) "Deutschland über Alles"

separatist ideal" with "increasing zeal during the last twenty years."[32]

The attack was renewed in a small book, *Their True Faith and Allegiance,* which Ohlinger wrote shortly afterward. On this occasion he was joined by Owen Wister, who lent his distinguished pen to the cause of loyalty in the form of a preface, in which, *inter alia,* he repeated Le Queux's story of the Potsdam meeting of 1908. In his text Ohlinger took great pains to demonstrate that the Alliance was the instrument of Pan-Germanism in America. He also dealt at some length with the spread of *Kultur* and the German-American entry into politics. Under the slogan "Use the ballot for your *Deutschtum,*" he asserted, the German-Americans were organizing to carry the election of 1916 in the interest of Germany:

. . . "We must forget party," said Congressman Bartholdt, "and without regard for previous affiliations vote only for those men who are the friends of Germanism."

His words were echoed by members of the Alliance from coast to coast.[33]

A final journalistic shot was fired, on the eve of the election, by Frank Perry Olds in an article on " 'Kultur' in American Politics" in the *Atlantic Monthly* of September, 1916. Olds was editor of the *Milwaukee Journal,* and could profess some knowledge of the German-American movement

does not mean "Germany *over* everything else" but "Germany *before* everything else" — that is, loyalty to the Reich before loyalty to the various territories, Bavaria, Saxony, Prussia, and so on. Here the forger seems to have stumbled over his own ignorance. The boast about ruling the United States is a little too bombastic to be in any way convincing. The "high decoration" to which the kaiser allegedly referred was actually a mere "fourth-class" German order given to Hexamer in recognition of his work in connection with the German theater in Philadelphia. Surely the man who ruled the United States in the interests of the German Empire deserved something a little better than this (which was, after all, rather like a great university honoring a distinguished foreign statesman with an honorary B.A. degree!).

[32] Gustavus Ohlinger, "German Propaganda in the United States," *Atlantic Monthly,* 117:535–547 (April, 1916).

[33] Gustavus Ohlinger, *Their True Faith and Allegiance* (1916), xv, 96–98.

in the Middle West. His article dealt mainly with certain activities of the Alliance, with reference to the election of 1916, which we shall consider in a later chapter. The aim of these he characterized (with some vagueness, perhaps) as "Kultur": "The Alliance further admits that it has been trying to consolidate the German vote. . . . Such consolidation of the German vote, taken together with the admitted aims of the Alliance, can aim at but one thing: permanent legislation in favor of "Kultur" and a pro-German policy in our international dealings."[34]

The campaign against the hyphen was accompanied by a certain amount of persecution from official quarters. On March 8, 1916, Alphonse G. Koelble complained that "the President of the United States, the secret service, and the British spies" were all working together against him: "my every movement is watched; my mail is opened by the secret service of this Government." When on May 1 the Alliance arranged a meeting for Professor Kühnemann at Hackensack, New Jersey, the local school board, which provided the auditorium, insisted upon having German-speaking police there to see that nothing was said which was unfriendly to "President Wilson, Congress, the United States, or the flag." Detectives were present at the annual convention of the New York State Alliance at Buffalo on July 2 and 3. Thus to place any movement under police supervision was the surest way to make its aims look criminal. Members of the Alliance who were in government service found it advisable to weigh their words carefully. Early in May Ernst Bruncken, German-American historian and a member of the German Societies of Washington, D.C., was dismissed from his post as assistant registrar of copyrights for remarks alleged to have been insulting to "President Wilson, the United States, and the American people." Complaints were also made on August 30 that Ger-

[34] Frank Perry Olds, " 'Kultur' in American Politics," in the *Atlantic Monthly*, 108:382–391 (September, 1916).

man-Americans were being dismissed from the mine-layer *Ringold*.[35]

On June 17, 1916, there came another demand for the suppression of the Alliance. For some time a campaign had been waged against the German-Americans in the press by one Maurice Leon, a native of Syria. Described by the *Times* as an "eminent lawyer," Leon gave his address, significantly enough, as Wall Street. According to the German-language papers, he was a professional propagandist, the "Syrian-born agent of the French government."[36] Early in 1915 he had entered into bitter controversy with Bartholdt over the Delbrück Law and had charged that it was "unsafe to naturalize Germans."[37] In a letter to the Philadelphia *Public Ledger* he now called upon the president and the Democratic Party to revoke the charter of the Alliance on the grounds that it was a "disloyal conspiracy" in the interests of Germany.[38]

To Leon's charges Hexamer made, on June 19, a spirited reply. He denied that at any time, directly or indirectly, had the Alliance had any dealings with a European power. To prove the truth of this statement he invited Congress to investigate its activities since the beginning of the war. Throughout June and July a cross-fire of correspondence went on in the press between Hexamer and Leon. The Philadelphia *Public Ledger* found itself the constant battleground between the hyphen and its assailants, and an occasional fray reached Congress itself, when one side or the other sought to enlist its sympathies. Leon stood inexorably by the charges made in the *World* exposé of March 7. He emphasized the at-

[35] *World,* March 9, 1916; *Times,* May 1, 6, 1916; *New-Yorker Staats-Zeitung,* July 3, August 31, 1916. The headlines over the *Times* story of Bruncken's dismissal are suggestive—"Wilson Critic Loses Job." May 6, 1916.

[36] *Times,* July 7, 1916; *Germania-Herold,* July 10, 1916.

[37] *America and the War,* letters and comments written for publication in the press and reprinted by Maurice Leon, Wall Street, New York, 1915, pp. 1–15. See also the *Literary Digest,* 50:42–43 (January 9, 1915), and *Fatherland,* vol. 2, no. 2, p. 7 (February 17, 1915).

[38] Quoted in the *New-Yorker Staats-Zeitung,* June 20, 1916.

titude taken by the Democratic National Convention with reference to combinations of persons conspiring against the government and urged that the party should make the Alliance a test case.[39]

On the other hand, there is little evidence that the Alliance was afraid of his charges. It pressed vigorously for a public inquiry into its loyalty. At the annual convention of the Wisconsin Alliance at Marshfield on July 23, 1916, Leo Stern expressed the wish that Congress would take up the matter immediately.[40] The Alliance of Elizabeth, New Jersey, on the twenty-fourth, called upon Senators Hughes and Martine and Congressman Capstick to lend their support to the idea of an investigation. To which the editor of *The Fatherland* added: "By all means let us have a Congressional investigation and get at the truth of the question who is creating mistrust and suspicion in the rank and file of the American people, and what is at the bottom of their activity."[41]

In retort to the charges of "hyphenism" the German-Americans revived the epithets of "Knownothingism" and "Nativism" for their opponents.[42] They warned against the dangers of intolerance, and openly accused the hyphen-baiters of hypocrisy. While many supporters of the Allies, among them Eliot of Harvard, William J. White, and Theodore Roosevelt, had publicly pleaded for an entente with Great Britain, the bulletin of the Alliance pointed out in January, 1916, not one of the German-American leaders had even suggested that the United States enter the war on the side of Germany.[43]

[39] *Ibid.*, June 20, 1916; *Illinois Staats-Zeitung* (Chicago), June 20, 1916; *Times*, July 7, 1916.
[40] "Dann werde es sich ja herausstellen, dass diese gemeinen und böswilligen Angriffe jedes Grundes entbehren." *Germania-Herold*, July 24, 1916.
[41] *New York Times*, July 25, 1916; *Fatherland*, vol. 4, no. 23, p. 363 (July 12, 1916).
[42] See, for example, Professor Julius Goebel, "Das wiederbelebte Knownothingtum," in Singer's *Jahrbuch*, 1916, pp. 97–103.
[43] *Mitteilungen*, January, 1916, pp. 4–5.

Demonstrations and pledges of loyalty were made by the various branches of the Alliance. At the annual convention of the Iowa Alliance at Davenport on March 17 and 18, 1916, it was resolved that the German-American would live up to his oath of allegiance even though "he may be forced by a partial government with bleeding heart to fight for England." On June 4 the Alliance and other organizations arranged a Liberty Day procession of 160,000 in New York. At the mass demonstration which followed, it was declared that every attempt to divide Americans on racial lines "should be abhorrent to all, and politicians who seek to influence the unthinking on this question in order to curry favor with those who are brought to question our Americanism, should be repudiated at the polls." In a Flag Day speech, delivered before the Betsy Ross House in Philadelphia, Hexamer reminded the country of the services rendered by the German-Americans in the past, adding:

Those who perchance finding themselves today in power and influential position, and who for one reason or another are attacking some of their own countrymen and fellow-citizens, insinuating that, because they are of a birth or extraction other than themselves, they are therefore a distinct and undesirable group, are committing a crime against the life of our body politic and are shaking the very foundations upon which our Republic rests.[44]

As we shall see later, Wilson also used the occasion of June 14 to deal with the hyphen issue and again to arraign the loyalty of some German-Americans. His speech brought a sharp protest from Henry Weismann, who characterized his reluctance to allow the German-Americans to differ with him on questions of foreign policy as "quite an innovation and a mighty dangerous one." This was a time of considerable tension between the United States and Mexico, when the

[44] *Ibid.*, April, 1916, p. 13; *Fatherland*, vol. 4, no. 19, p. 294 (June 14, 1916); vol. 4, no. 20, p. 311 (June 21, 1916); *New-Yorker Staats-Zeitung*, June 5, 16, 1916; *Hearings on the German-American Alliance*, 368–369.

attack of a Carranzist force upon Pershing's column on June 21 threatened to precipitate a war. Thus when the New York Alliance convened at Buffalo on July 3, it endeavored to exemplify its loyalty by pledging to the country the life and property of each of its members. Already Alphonse G. Koelble had signified the readiness of the United German Societies of New York City to enlist for the war, and members of the Alliance of Elizabeth, New Jersey, were planning the formation of a volunteer regiment.[45]

Many other state conventions of the Alliance held during that summer dealt at length with the hyphen question and issued some specific pledge of loyalty. The Alliance of South Dakota expressed regret that the loyalty of one section of the American population should, "in these critical days, when our nation stands more than ever in need of unity," be impugned for refusing to follow "blindly a political leadership" in which it could not conscientiously concur. At its convention at Marshfield on July 23 the Wisconsin Alliance voiced its indignation in a long "Declaration of Principles":

When our government, by its servility to another power, injures the pride and honor of this country and constantly exerts its influence for the benefit of this foreign power; when the same government replies to the continued attacks upon the rights and interests of our nation only with feeble representations and never with a real and energetic protest; when the same government, by its consent to the sale of arms and ammunition to one side only of the nations involved in the war, makes itself guilty of a breach of neutrality; when the same government, by fostering a pseudo-Americanism, seeks to sow hate and dissension among our citizens, — then we consider it not only our right, but also our duty as patriotic citizens, to make a stand against these acts and to throw our influence into the balance to get the situation changed.[46]

[45] *Times*, June 18, 23, 27, July 4, 1916; *Germania-Herold*, July 4, 1916; *New-Yorker Staats-Zeitung*, July 4, 1916; *World*, July 5, 1916. Mayor Mitchell expressed disapproval of the formation of German regiments in New York. *Times*, June 28, 1916.
[46] *Milwaukee-Sonntagspost*, July 23, 1916; *Germania-Herold*, July 24, 1916.

Any man, declared Judge John Schwaab at the annual convention of the Ohio Alliance on August 18, who could betray the land of his birth could also betray the United States. Sympathy for the German cause went hand in hand in the case of the German-Americans with loyalty to the United States. In any case, asserted a resolution passed by the Missouri Alliance at Hermann on September 25, it was they who gloried in the name "Anglo-Saxon" who were the oldest hyphen-bearers in this country.[47]

As further evidence of their loyalty many branches of the Alliance joined in the general demand for preparedness, and this despite their suspicion that the whole movement might be aimed at Germany. As early as December 17, 1915, in a letter to C. A. Ryan of the World Peace Association, Hexamer had admitted some reforms in the national defense system to be necessary, expressing at the same time a fear that an organized preparedness movement might be a subsidiary of the "Anglo-American Money Trust." The New York Alliance at its Buffalo convention of July 3, 1916, "joined itself heartily" with those who demanded a better condition of national preparedness. The South Dakota Alliance quoted and indorsed George Washington to the effect that to be prepared was the surest way to keep the peace. The Central Alliance of Pennsylvania, on August 6, pledged itself for "reasonable preparedness, based upon patriotism . . . but free from politics and jingoism." The Alliance of Nebraska followed in September with a similar declaration.[48]

The campaign against the hyphen was a significant, if not altogether creditable, chapter of American history in the war years. Perhaps it contained some slight element of sincerity for those who were concerned with it. Perhaps even so highly intelligent a person as President Wilson could honestly be-

[47] *Germania-Herold,* August 30, 1916; *Westliche Post* (St. Louis), September 26, 1916.
[48] *New-Yorker Staats-Zeitung,* July 4, December 18, 1916; *Times,* July 4, 1916; *Milwaukee-Sonntagspost,* July 23, October 1, 1916; *Germania-Herold,* August 7, 1916.

lieve that a number of the German-Americans were flagrantly disloyal. But for the most part one cannot escape the conclusion that it was just good politics, that its chief purpose was to discredit the German-Americans in view of the part which they were bound to play in the election of 1916. Apart from Colonel Roosevelt, the movement had a decidedly Democratic, pro-administration flavor. If it could be shown that the German-Americans were disloyal, and that their stand in the election was determined solely by their devotion to the interests of Germany, then there would be a landslide of pro-Ally and pro-American votes for the candidate to whom they were opposed. Thus as the campaign progressed there was, as we shall see, a tendency on the part of certain persons connected with the government to glory in the fact that the German-Americans were against them.

VI

THE ELECTION OF 1916

By VIRTUE OF ITS EVER DEEPENING ENGULFMENT IN LOCAL AND national politics on the question of prohibition, the Alliance had tended to become at times little more than a non-partisan political organization. To defeat prohibition it had become associated with political deals which, even as political deals go, were of questionable honesty; and to make itself more effective politically it had accepted subsidies which to even the most cynical of its leaders must have appeared a little inconsistent with the high cultural purpose for which it was founded. Yet, in striking contrast to its attitude on prohibition, it had always professed an aversion to politics as such. In the constitution which it adopted in 1901 it announced its firm intention to "refrain from participation in party politics."[1] On July 4, 1903, it published a "Political Declaration of Independence of the German-Americans," in which it stated its firm purpose not to become the tool of the politicians.[2] In 1907 it accepted a charter from Congress, which of course deprived it of all legal right to take part in politics.

The name of its president, Dr. Hexamer, was twice mentioned in Pennsylvania for the office of governor, but he unhesitatingly declined the honor.[3] In February, 1915, a suggestion that he run for president, with the object of taking the Irish and German votes from the regular parties, was rejected with equal firmness.[4] His decision was loudly applauded by the National Alliance. "Politics corrupts charac-

[1] Heinrici, *Das Buch der Deutschen in Amerika*, 781–782.
[2] *German-American Annals*, 1903, pp. 436–437.
[3] *Milwaukee-Sonntagspost*, November 15, 1914.
[4] *Mitteilungen*, March, 1915, p. 28. "Dr. Hexamer sind wiederholt Kandidaturen angetragen worden . . . Er hat sie stets abgelehnt."—*Note of the editor.*

ter," announced its press bureau in November, 1914, in discussing one of the earlier offers of political honors, "and political ambitions on the part of the leaders of the German-American movement would rob them of their usefulness. . . . Political aspirations must be kept outside the National Alliance, the state Alliances, and the branches."[5]

Even after the outbreak of the war the German-Americans were rarely flattered when their support, as such, was solicited by politicians. This was the unhappy experience of Robert M. Sweitzer, a candidate for mayor in Chicago in February, 1915, who was widely advertised as "the German candidate" and as "blood of our blood," but who found himself repudiated by the German element at the polls.[6] Nor did the occasional talk of forming a "German Party" ever meet with any encouragement from the German-American leaders, who were only too well aware of the unwillingness of the rest of the nation to tolerate anything of the sort.[7] Thus when in March, 1915, the Central Verein of Passaic, New Jersey, suggested the idea, Richard Bartholdt used all his influence against it.[8]

Yet even Bartholdt was of the opinion that in future it was the duty of the German-Americans "to put on jack-boots, instead of creeping around in gum-shoes" in national affairs.[9] With the approach of the election of 1916 many other prominent German-Americans came to the conclusion that the only way to make themselves heard on questions of peace and neutrality was to enter the political arena on an impressive scale. They viewed with considerable uneasiness the pos-

[5] "Dieselben müssen auf einer parteilosen Basis stehen und keine anderen Beweggründe für Unterstützung von Kandidaten kennen als deren liberale Gesinnung und deren Anerkennung deutscher Verdienste und Kulturbestrebungen." *Milwaukee-Sonntagspost,* November 15, 1914.
[6] See the advertisement in the *Illinois Staats-Zeitung* (Chicago), February 18, 1915.
[7] See the suggestion made at a meeting of the Verband deutscher Chordirigenten at Philadelphia, in the *Milwaukee-Sonntagspost,* October 18, 1914; also *New Yorker Kampf um Wahrheit und Frieden,* p. 26, and the *Illinois Staats-Zeitung,* September 17, 1914.
[8] *Mitteilungen,* April, 1915, pp. 15–16.   [9] *Ibid.,* 16.

sible re-election of Wilson. To some extent they were actuated by a desire to punish him. But more important it was
that they bring about a change in American policy. This
meant the election of a president, as they expressed it, who
would enforce American rights with equal severity against
both belligerents, and who would be partial to neither.

Wilson's renomination by the Democratic Party was a foregone conclusion. It therefore remained for the German-
Americans to concentrate primarily upon the Republicans.
Their chief task was to make it clear which nominations they
would, and which they would not, be prepared to support.
With several candidates in the field, it was quite likely that
their choice might tip the scales in favor of a suitable man.
In any case the Republicans could not ignore their wishes
entirely, for in view of their strong opposition to Wilson it
was obvious that unless some deliberate move were made to
discourage them, they would gravitate in large numbers toward the Republican side.

Elihu Root, one possibility, was strenuously opposed on
account of his pro-Ally sympathies. But the real *bête noir*
in the Republican camp was Theodore Roosevelt. Roosevelt
was not only pro-Ally, but was one of the chief sponsors of
the campaign against the hyphen. His attacks upon the
German-Americans had become violent even to the point of
recklessness. He seemed to glory in the use of the strongest
political invective against them, and was unrepentent in the
face of all their protests. "Thank Heaven," he wrote to Henry
Cabot Lodge, on February 18, 1915, "I no longer have to
consider the effect of my actions upon any party; and accordingly I have temperately, but with the strongest emphasis, attacked the German-American propaganda and the effort
by the German-Americans to use the United States as an
instrument in the interest of Germany."[10]

---

[10] *Correspondence of Roosevelt and Lodge*, 2:456–457. According to a statement by Judge John Schwaab of the Ohio Alliance, Roosevelt contemptuously
suggested on one occasion that "In God we trust" on American coins should

For this stand Roosevelt found his name struck off one after another of the many German-American clubs which, in the cordial years of his presidency, had elected him to honorary membership. The bulletin of the Alliance came out bitterly against him. After one of his anti-German speeches at Plattsburg on August 25, 1915, it shuddered to think that such a man "not long ago stood at the head of our national government," and denounced him as a bigger demagogue than the "Italian mountebank D'Annunzio." In November it charged him with being in the pay of Great Britain through his connection with the *Outlook,* arguing that the latter was subsidized with British money, and that he was drawing a hundred thousand dollars a year from it. What was really worrying both president and former president, it added, was the fact that neither could expect to receive German-American support for public office again. "Certainly it cannot be pleasant to these gentlemen to see that the Americans of German descent are becoming more and more a factor in political life, because they represent in its truest form the American ideal of liberty, and use their influence solely to preserve the United States, not only from foreign entanglements, but also from a return to its former dependence upon England."[11]

An attempt to reconcile the German-Americans to Roosevelt met with conspicuous failure. Such an attempt was made by Professor Hugo Münsterberg of Harvard, an old friend of the colonel's, who thought he would be the best man to bring the European war to a quick end, and who distrusted all the other Republican possibilities. Münsterberg arranged a meeting between Roosevelt and George Sylvester Viereck of *The Fatherland.* This came to nought when Roosevelt refused to be moved from his anti-German position and con-

be replaced by "To Hell with the Hyphen." *Mitteilungen,* December, 1915, p. 33.
    [11] *Times,* May 15, 1915; *Mitteilungen,* September, 1915, p. 43; November, 1915, p. 4.

tinued to argue, with every conviction, that the kaiser was plotting against the United States. Münsterberg also published an appeal for Roosevelt in the press: "The psychological equation of his personality makes him a pro-German in all that is best in him, and only his temper and his perpetual desire to be with the masses make him a pro-Ally."[12]

The documents published by the *World* in its exposé of March 7, 1916, indicated that even as early as November, 1915, the leaders of the Alliance had been discussing plans for the election—although not exactly along the lines described by that newspaper. At that time, it will be recalled, Hexamer was in Wisconsin on a propaganda tour, during which he outlined one of the several political schemes which have borne the name of the "Wisconsin Idea." The "Idea" was the result of considerable deliberation. It was assumed that Wilson could not fail to be renominated, and it was feared that he would receive the votes of many pro-Ally Republicans, as well as of the Democrats. "A Republican victory under these conditions," it was concluded, "is only possible if a candidate is set up who is conservative in his principles, who only shows and sanctions real neutral views, and who shall express neither pro-British, nor pro-German, but only pro-American tendencies." To guarantee that only such a candidate be elected it was proposed that a portion of the delegates to the Republican National Convention—"a quarter to a third"—should consist of distinguished German-Americans.[13] The leaders of the Alliance should confer at once with the chairmen of the Republican state committees, and make their bargains on the basis of German-American

[12] George S. Viereck, *The Strangest Friendship in History, W. Wilson and E. M. House* (Liveright, New York, 1932), 161; *Fatherland,* vol. 3, no. 20, pp. 345–348 (December 22, 1915). See the comment which Münsterberg's appeal aroused, in the *Literary Digest,* 52:3–4 (January 1, 1916).

[13] This would hardly constitute an attempt to "control" the convention, as the editor of the *World* argued in his exposé of March 7, for "distinguished German-Americans" did not necessarily mean officers of the Alliance.

representation in return for the promise of German-American support. In Wisconsin the German-Americans had already been conceded ten of the twenty-six Republican delegates. "If in a majority of the states, this number could be secured, only such a candidate would be selected as would represent the neutral American situation which we desire."[14]

The "Idea" was impractical and absurd, as some were soon to perceive. When it was submitted to Bartholdt, one of the few German-American leaders with any very wide political experience, he definitely discouraged it. Having recently attended a meeting of the Republican National Committee in Washington he was conscious of a disinclination, at that early date, to cater to the German vote, and frankly admitted that he could get "but little satisfaction." "Party men," he added, "who have achieved the distinction of being big enough to be selected as delegates to a national convention are mighty scarce among the Germans." As an alternative Bartholdt suggested that the German-Americans might start a "Champ Clark boom" among the Democrats. Although a Republican, he himself (for such was apparently the nature of politics in Missouri, whence he was writing) "could probably set something in motion here."[15]

Henry Weismann also was enough of a realist to see that in any arrangement which the Alliance concluded with the Republican Party the latter was bound to get the best of the bargain. The type of men acceptable to the one would not be acceptable to the other. Those German-Americans who might finally be selected could not be relied upon to "have stamina enough to stand for our ideas." And in any case "they would not accord us representation unless we were willing to abide by the results of the convention." Hence there was very little enthusiasm for the "Idea" outside Wis-

[14] The "Idea" is outlined in a letter from Leo Stern to Koelble (written some time toward the end of 1915). See the *World*, March 7, 1916. See also George S. Viereck, *Spreading Germs of Hate* (Liveright, New York, 1930), 241.
[15] Bartholdt to Koelble, December 21, 28, 1915, in the *World*, March 7, 1916.

consin, and even there it was never carried through success-
fully.[16]

In the end a considerable amount of local political organization on the part of the state Alliances and branches pre-
ceded any successful form of national regimentation. The
Middle West steeled itself particularly hard for the occasion.
In January, 1916, the Milwaukee Alliance, anxious to mobilize all its possible strength, urged all Germans who were
eligible to take out their citizenship papers "in view of the
hard political battle now in sight." In March the executive
committee of the Illinois Alliance held a special meeting to
deal with the forthcoming political conventions. At this meeting it adopted the slogan *Alle gegen Roosevelt und Wilson.*
It also issued a manifesto to its branches in which it sought
to show that the German vote could hold the balance of
power between the two major parties. "It forms, in a sense,
the tongue of the wagon: if the German vote swings to one
side, the other is lost beyond hope, as has been proved in
earlier elections . . . If the German-Americans begin a
powerful agitation now, it may be expected that at least one
of the parties will see the handwriting on the wall and nominate a truly American candidate."[17]

On March 6 the Minnesota Alliance drew up a circular
for the guidance of its members, telling them how to use
their influence in the election of delegates to the conventions, and giving the names of candidates to be supported.
At its annual convention at Davenport, on March 17 and
18, the Iowa Alliance announced that the German-American
would "do all in his power to see that the next administration will be American—neither pro-British, nor pro-German,

[16] Weismann to Koelble, December 22, 1915, in the *World*, March 7, 1916. See
the report from Milwaukee, March 8: "The German Plan to control the
Wisconsin Republican National Convention delegation is admitted here, but
it failed because Alvin Kletzsch was not able to put through his scheme to
have the state committee name the delegation." *Times*, March 9, 1916.
[17] *Hearings on the German-American Alliance,* 122; *Mitteilungen,* April,
1916, p. 18; May, 1916, p. 15.

but only a truly American administration," and decided to "oppose . . . with every honest means at its disposal" the nomination and election of Wilson and Roosevelt. Prohibition, it was added, "so long one of our chief cares, is now a secondary issue—there is something more important at stake: the preservation of the best of Americanism, of which we German-Americans, despite the hyphen, or perhaps on account of it, consider ourselves a part."[18]

In the far West the California Alliance met on February 28 to discuss the election. At the time it failed to obtain any unanimity; one speaker, Daniel O'Connell of the American Independence Union, even urged the German-Americans to register as Democrats on the grounds that it was the Republicans who were behind Wilson's "anti-German" policy. At a meeting of the Oregon Alliance on April 1 an opposite view prevailed. Ernst Kroner of the American Neutrality League, although himself a Democrat, urged all German-Americans to affiliate with the Republicans, for it was Wilson who was "intent upon the annihilation of the German-American cause in the United States." This suggestion was indorsed by F. H. Dammasch, president of the Alliance, and was adopted as the policy of the branch.[19]

In the East the Central Alliance of Pennsylvania sent out, in March, an appeal to all its branches to make sure that the entire German element registered for the primaries. At the same time the Allegheny County Alliance began to indicate a curious preference for Henry Ford as its presidential candidate. On April 2 the New Jersey Alliance met for its annual convention at Elizabeth. Here Mayor Mravlag, a native of Austria, aroused adverse comment when, in welcoming the delegates, he stated that "if they planned to criticize the Administration, they should do so only as Americans." His speech anticipated the main business of the convention,

[18] *Hearings on the German-American Alliance,* 107; *Mitteilungen,* April, 1916, p. 13.
[19] *Ibid.,* April, 1916, p. 18; May, 1916, p. 21.

which was to be a discussion of the election. Reported to be the most important meeting ever held by the state Alliance, it was marked by unusually animated debates. Party loyalties became obvious when some delegates refused to lay the sole blame for the anti-hyphen campaign upon Wilson. In the end a majority agreed upon a resolution "against Wilson, Roosevelt, and Root" and an appeal to the members "to agitate against the nomination of such candidates with all the resources at their command." It was also decided that henceforth the executive committee of the Alliance should meet twice monthly, one meeting to be devoted entirely to election questions.[20]

Meanwhile the *World* had gone to some trouble and expense to follow carefully the activities of the various branches of the Alliance. On May 7 it published reports from special correspondents who had been sent out to gather information. From Chicago it was reported that the Illinois Alliance, claiming to represent seventy-five thousand votes, was co-operating solidly with the Teutonic Sons of America against the re-election of Wilson. The German-language newspapers, the *Illinois Staats-Zeitung, Abendpost,* and *Freie Presse,* were equally opposed to Wilson, and it was predicted that if the Republicans should perchance nominate Roosevelt, the German vote would go to the Socialists. In Ohio the Alliance had not as yet clarified its position. In Missouri seventy-five per cent of the German-Americans were said to be Republicans in any case, and in St. Louis "controlled the elective offices of the city." The Missouri Alliance, it was reported, was "very active" for the Republicans. The correspondent at Des Moines, Iowa, wrote that "the German-American Alliance is a political organization, pure and simple." The Minnesota Alliance, though standing firmly with the rest against Wilson, was found to be reconcilable to

[20] *Ibid.,* April, 1916, p. 25; *Hearings on the German-American Alliance,* 320; *Times,* April 3, 1916; *New-Yorker Staats-Zeitung,* April 3, 1916.

Root, who in the words of its president, Julius Moersch, was considered to have "a reputation for that sort of firmness which the German people applauds."[21]

Warnings that these Alliances might be overhasty in their political decisions had already been heard in certain quarters. Henry Weismann repeatedly exerted his influence in favor of caution and conservatism. In a circular of December, 1915, he asked the branches of the New York Alliance not to place the names and addresses of their members at the disposal of politicians seeking advancement in the election of 1916. In a letter to the *New-Yorker Staats-Zeitung* in March, 1916, he came out strongly against the entente with the Republicans. "Although I am, under normal conditions, a Republican, I must nevertheless confess that the Republicans, in and out of Congress, especially those of the Eastern states, have displayed, and are still displaying, a greater servility to the munitions and finance kings than the Democrats, including the president. . . . There is more to fear from this section, which holds the reins in the party, than from Democracy." On April 25 he told a reporter of the *World* that it should be left to every individual German-American to make his own choice and that so far as he was concerned the relations between the United States and Germany would play no part in the coming campaign. Even after many branches had definitely committed themselves to a course of political action, he made, at the annual convention at Buffalo on July 2, a determined effort to keep the New York Alliance out of the presidential campaign.[22]

To many German-Americans, however, the election of 1916 was, in the words of the St. Louis *Westliche Post*, "the most important election since 1860." Even as far back as March 6, 1915, the *Literary Digest*, in discussing "German-American Distrust of the Administration" had predicted that

---

[21] All the reports are published in the *World*, May 7, 1916.
[22] *World*, March 7, April 26, July 3, 1916; *Mitteilungen*, April, 1916, p. 22; *New-Yorker Staats-Zeitung*, July 3, 1916.

"if German-American feeling plays a part in politics we may
have a new 'issue' here for 1916." There was for the most
part every intention on the part of the branches of the Alliance of taking a very active interest. At this time the Alliance was nationally still on the ascendant, having increased
its membership considerably since the outbreak of the war.
It had every confidence that it could make its power a somewhat unpleasant surprise to its opponents. On March 7
Hexamer's secretary is reported to have told the press that
it would exert all its influence in the election. Nothing, declared *Mitteilungen* in April, would be at that time more
cowardly and unworthy than "to grovel in fear before the
pro-British press." The importance of taking part in the primaries was urged at the same time by Adolph Timm, the
national secretary, who also requested all the branches to
draw the attention of their members and others to registra-
tion and voting days. The political strength of the German-
Americans was growing, it was asserted in the Milwaukee
Germania-Herold of May 4. Washington had awakened to
the fact that they were taking a keen interest in national affairs, and there were "headaches in the White House."[23]

By virtue of its charter the National Alliance was prevented from any direct participation in the election. There
were already threats of legal proceedings against it for what
had been done so far, especially in Pennsylvania, where
Hexamer was summoned by the district attorney of Pittsburgh to appear before a grand jury and answer for himself
and his fellow officers. Serious complications were avoided
when the Central Alliance of Pennsylvania came forward to
assume the political leadership of the German-Americans
and thereby to draw the fire of the opponents. The Central
Alliance of Pennsylvania was, as we have seen, the parent of
the National Alliance, but had remained an unincorporated

[23] *Westliche Post* (St. Louis), October 4, 1916; *Literary Digest,* 50:465 (March
6, 1915); *Times,* March 8, 1916; *Mitteilungen,* April, 1916, pp. 4–5, 7; *Germania-
Herold,* May 4, 1916.

organization. Its legislative committee had already achieved some political distinction in the fight against prohibition, and it was in a strong position to take the lead in 1916. Its secretary, Adolph Timm, was also secretary of the National Alliance, which was considerably to its advantage.[24]

On April 16, 1916, the legislative committee of the Central Alliance of Pennsylvania met in special session at Altoona. Here plans were made for a national conference of all German-American organizations "to give expression to the views of the whole German element with reference to certain presidential candidates in the right manner and at the right place." The conference was to appoint a committee to make known its views at the national political conventions. It was to meet in some mid-Western city toward the end of May.[25]

An invitation to participate in the conference was issued on May 1 by John B. Mayer and Adolf Timm "to the executive committees of the state Alliances of the National German-American Alliance; to the German clubs; to the German fraternal associations; to war veterans; to societies of singers and *Turners;* to organizations of men of all religious confessions, and to the representatives of the German-language press." This invitation stated that the aim of the conference would be to make known the wishes of the German-Americans "clearly and unmistakably to the powers that be, either before or on the days of meeting of the conventions of both political parties." The conference was to meet at Chicago on May 28 and 29.[26]

[24] *New-Yorker Staats-Zeitung,* April 20, 1916.

[25] *Ibid.,* April 20, 1916.

[26] *Mitteilungen,* May, 1916, p. 6; *Germania-Herold* (Milwaukee), May 4, 1916; *New-Yorker Staats-Zeitung,* May 4, 1916. Carl Wittke *(German-Americans and the World War,* 90) writes as if the "Wisconsin Idea" were contemporaneous with the Chicago conference: "Simultaneously, the 'Wisconsin Idea' was suggested, a plan to elect German-American delegates to the Republican Convention." Actually, as we have seen, the "Idea" was conceived in November, 1915, and had by this time been proved impractical. Had it succeeded there would not have been the same necessity for the Chicago conference.

Although the best response came from the state Alliances and their branches, there were numerous delegations from other German-American groups. All denominations of the German-American churches were represented. Sixty German-language newspapers lent their support, as did also the National German-American Publishers' Association, which had been formed on February 27 to promote uniformity of opinion on national questions and to prevent the nomination of Wilson, Roosevelt, and Root.[27] Among the prominent German-Americans who attended were Joseph Frey, president of the Roman Catholic Central Verein; Pastor Siegmund G. von Bosse, of the Philadelphia German Conference of the Lutheran Church and also of the Delaware Alliance; Max Hottelet of Milwaukee, president of the German War Veterans; Jakob Willig, the *Turner* leader; and many officers of the German-American Alliances. Twenty-eight states were represented directly among the Alliance delegates, and fourteen more by proxy. Yet the conference claimed to be nothing more than the spontaneous effort of patriotic American citizens. "The representatives of the various societies, church congregations, lodges, etc.," it was reported from Philadelphia, where both the National Alliance and the Pennsylvania Central Alliance had their headquarters, "will not confer as such, but as American citizens, who have the welfare of this country at heart, and who desire that their voices shall be heard as much as those of others."[28]

When on the morning of May 28 the delegates assembled in the Hotel Kaiserhof for their first session, John B. Mayer opened the meeting with an appeal for a few seconds of complete silence, and then declared dramatically: "Gentlemen: Let this meeting sink deep into your memories. It stands alone in the history of the German element in this country.

[27] *New-Yorker Staats-Zeitung*, May 25, 1916. See also *ibid.*, February 28, 1916.
[28] *Germania-Herold*, May 29, 1916; *Milwaukee-Sonntagspost*, August 6, 1916. *Germania-Herold*, May 25, 29, 1916. Wisconsin alone sent forty delegates.

We are proud to have been able to take part in it." He then went on to express resentment at the hyphen-baiting of recent months, and to urge that the German-Americans retaliate "with the weapon given to them as American citizens— the ballot slip." Messages of support were then read from all parts of the country, great applause greeting an ardent rimester of the far West who telegraphed: "Our glorious Union forever: Wilson and Roosevelt never."[29]

At the first session, which was held behind closed doors, the German-American Publishers submitted a political creed which received the unanimous indorsement of the conference. This condemned the fomenting of racial antipathies on the hyphen issue, and pronounced a ban on "all demogogues who seek to profit by national antipathies, and who try to extol their own loyalty by impugning that of others." It then asserted its faith in "frank diplomacy and international good-will, as opposed to the double standard in foreign relations which judges with harsh acerbity the mistakes of one nation, and condones with academic disapproval the offenses of another." It declared for the vigorous assertion of all American rights abroad and against any policy which would allow the United States to become the "partisan and henchman" of a foreign nation. "Adequate preparedness" was also favored.[30]

The conference then proceeded to clarify its own views on the forthcoming election. It discussed what it considered to be a proper policy for the United States in international affairs, and decided to support as president any man who would pursue such a policy. Its decisions were set forth in a series of eight resolutions, which were published in English and German in the German-language press on the following day. These constituted the "Chicago Platform" and were as follows:

[29] *Volksblatt und Freiheits-Freund* (Pittsburgh), June 4, 1915; Singer's *Jahrbuch*, 1917, p. 146; *New-Yorker Staats-Zeitung*, May 29, 1916.
[30] Singer's *Jahrbuch*, 147; *Fatherland* vol. 4, no. 18, p. 279 (June 7, 1916); *Times*, May 29, 1916; *Germania-Herold*, May 29, 1916.

We, the delegated representatives of more than 2,000,000 voters of the United States, in conference on May 29, resolve the following:

1. We demand a neutrality that corresponds to the counsel which George Washington gave the American people in his farewell address.

2. We urge a foreign policy which defends with equal firmness and justice the existence of American interests.

3. We condemn every official procedure and every policy which shows inherent sympathy toward one belligerent nation and unmitigated antipathy toward another.

4. We deplore those speeches, made by public officials, or former public officials, which are intended to — or which serve to — produce a division among the American people on grounds of nationality.

5. We hope that no party will nominate a presidential candidate whose views could accentuate such a division.

6. We cherish the confidence that, in the Republican Convention, all elements in the party will unite on a candidate whose views will be in harmony with the principles hereby submitted.

7. We hope that the Democratic Party will bring forward a presidential candidate who holds similar views to those hereby submitted.

8. We declare that no presidential candidate who is not in harmony with the views hereby proclaimed is worthy of the support of free and independent voters.[31]

From the conference there emerged a so-called Conference Committee. It was proposed by State Senator Fellinger of Cleveland and was to pilot the German-American movement through the election campaign. Nationally it was to act as an intermediary between the German-American organizations and the leaders of the political parties; locally it was to assist in the establishment of further Conference

---

[31] *New-Yorker Staats-Zeitung*, May 30, 1916. There was a lively debate on the second resolution, which, in the opinion of some delegates, might be construed as an indorsement of Wilson's policy toward Germany. See the *Germania-Herold*, May 30, 1916. The conference is also reported in Singer's *Jahrbuch*, 1917, pp. 145–153.

Committees and promote uniformity of action and opinion among the German-Americans. Immediately after the national conventions had made their nominations the Conference Committee was to question the candidates as to their attitude on the eight resolutions of the Chicago conference, and then to publish their replies in the German-language press. Its chairman was John B. Mayer, and its secretary Pastor von Bosse. Other members were Joseph Frey of the Central Verein, Dr. Friedrich Bente of St. Louis, Adolph Timm of the Pennsylvania and National Alliances, and Ferdinand Walther of the Chicago Alliance.[32]

As Max Hottelet of the German War Veterans pointed out in an interview for the *Milwaukee Sentinel* of May 30, the conference had not declared for any particular presidential candidate. "Any good American is satisfactory to us, except Theodore Roosevelt. We could not consider him for one moment." (Wilson was equally unacceptable, he omitted to add.) It had merely described its ideal candidate and had left it open to the conventions to provide a man who would measure up to its standards. Yet it had tended to commit itself mainly to the Republicans. It had, as we have seen, "cherished the confidence" that they would provide a candidate after its own heart, but had merely "hoped" that the Democrats might do so.[33] And when the Republican National Convention was about to meet, it made a point of having its preferences clearly understood. From the Chicago conference a deputation of German-American newspaper men called upon Charles D. Hilles, chairman of the Republican National Committee, and delivered what the *New York Times* called "an anti-Roosevelt ultimatum." German-American support, Hilles was informed, would be forthcoming for Hughes, Sherman, Fairbanks, or any favorite son, but never for Roosevelt or Root.[34]

[32] *Germania-Herold*, May 30, 1916.   [33] See Resolutions 6 and 7.
[34] *Times*, May 31, 1916; *Hearings on the German-American Alliance*, 415.

While to the *New York Times* its promoters were but
"hopeless aliens, wearing the cloak of American citizenship
to stab America," the Chicago conference was hailed with
wild delight by the German-language press. If ever there was
an expression of German-American unanimity, declared the
New-Yorker Staats-Zeitung, this was surely it. Its decisions
"emanated from a healthy Americanism, which demands
justice and impartiality in national as in international affairs." Anyone, in the opinion of the *Illinois Staats-Zeitung*,
who opposed its principles might "still be a good political
partisan, but never a good American." The entire conference, added the Pittsburgh *Volksblatt und Freiheits-Freund*,
was "an act of self-defense against the 'pogromist morale'
which has entered America, by way of England, from dark-
est Russia."[35]

Technically the National Alliance had taken no part in
the conference. Nor was it showing any official preference
in the election. In its bulletin for April, 1916, Hexamer
warned all branches that Section 83 of the United States
Criminal Code made it illegal for any incorporated organization to engage in party politics, and that according to Section 37 of the same Code it was an offense to enter into a
conspiracy to circumvent any law of the United States. Thus
nothing could be undertaken by the national body. Local
Alliances, however, which had no charter, could act as they
pleased, and the National Alliance could claim no restrain-
ing jurisdiction over them. Hence on June 4, in a statement
issued to the German-language press, it was claimed that in
no way could the Chicago conference be regarded as the
work of the National Alliance. Those who attended "merely
satisfied one of the demands of their duty as citizens in as-

[35] "The German Convention," editorial in the *Times*, June 1, 1916; *New-
Yorker Staats-Zeitung*, May 30, 1916; *Illinois Staats-Zeitung*, June 1, 1916;
Volksblatt und Freiheits-Freund, May 30, 1916. See also the editorial, "Die
Platform der Deutschamerikaner," in the *New-Yorker Staats-Zeitung*, May 31,
1916.

sembling to make a stand with reference to certain questions which were agitating the whole American nation."[36]

There was not the slightest doubt, however, that, though the name of the National Alliance might not appear in politics, its influence was going to be thrown, without reserve, into the election. As early as March 1, 1914, in a letter to Percy Andreae, Hexamer had predicted that Wilson would never enjoy a second term without the German vote, and that the Alliance would "keep its political powder dry" for this occasion. On August 5, 1915, at a big parade in San Francisco in connection with the eighth convention, he had hinted that "at the polls we German-Americans will show what we are worth."[37]

Headlines in both the Milwaukee *Germania-Herold* and the *Illinois Staats-Zeitung* described the Chicago conference as "the Conference of the National Alliance" and the "Plan of the National Alliance." This would at least indicate that prominent German-Americans, such as the editors of these newspapers, tended to regard it as such. Adolph Timm, secretary of the Alliance, was one of the originators of the idea. Max Heinrici, press agent of the Alliance and editor of *Mitteilungen*, helped to advertise it and after it was over began to answer in the German-language press some of the attacks which were being made upon it. Furthermore, when Hexamer invited the state presidents to attend an executive meeting of the Alliance on November 26, 1916 (such as was always held in the years when there was no national convention), many declined on the grounds that they felt that the Chicago conference had served the purposes of such a meeting.[38]

[36] *Mitteilungen,* April, 1916, p. 7. *Milwaukee-Sonntagspost,* April 2, 1916; *Volksblatt und Freiheits-Freund,* June 4, 1916.

[37] *Hearings on the German-American Alliance,* 236; *World,* August 6, 1915.

[38] *Germania-Herold,* May 4, November 7, 1916; *Illinois Staats-Zeitung,* May 4, 28, 1916; *Milwaukee-Sonntagspost,* June 4, 1916. "Nationalbund rüstet" had been the title of an article describing the preparations for the conference in the *New-Yorker Staats-Zeitung,* April 20, 1916. Dr. Michael Singer also speaks of it as being summoned by the National Alliance. Singer's *Jahrbuch,* 1917, p. 30.

The man who felt himself most violently abused by the conference was Theodore Roosevelt. The German-language press claimed widely that it had defeated his last chances of nomination, and gloried in his disability.[39] Certain German-American leaders stated publicly that his nomination would mean the ruin of the Republican Party.[40] Roosevelt himself, although he must have realized that there were other factors precluding his nomination, attached considerable importance to the German-American opposition. On November 27, 1915, in a letter to Lodge, he stressed the fact that "the German-Americans, the professional hyphenated Americans of every kind, and the whole flapdoodle pacifist and mollycoddle outfit" would be against him. And, in subsequent letters:

As you know, I feel that the course I have followed about the hyphenated Americanism, and especially the German-American vote, is such as absolutely to preclude the possibility of nominating me as a candidate.

No politician desiring political preference would enter on a campaign to alienate the German-American vote and the pacifist vote and to wake up our people to unpleasant facts by telling them unpleasant truths. My judgment is now and has been from the beginning that this course would render me impossible as a candidate.[41]

[39] "It is to the Alliance that Roosevelt attributes his defeat for the Republican nomination," stated *Fatherland*, vol. 4, no. 24, pp. 376–377 (July 19, 1916). According to the same source, there was gossip in Washington that Ohlinger's book *Their True Faith and Allegiance* (see above, page 103) had been written in spite by Roosevelt, and that Ohlinger was a mere pseudonym. See also Singer's *Jahrbuch*, 1917, p. 150, and the resolution passed by the Illinois Alliance on September 11, 1916, in the *New-Yorker Staats-Zeitung*, September 12, 1916. Roosevelt, of course, was not the man to become chargrined at what the conference may have said about him, but he was resentful that such a conference, which he regarded as un-American, should have convened in an attempt to disqualify him and others for their anti-German and anti-German-American attitude.

[40] See, for example, the statement of Otto Koenig at a meeting of the Wisconsin Alliance in Milwaukee on June 2: "He is positively the last man any German would want to see nominated on the Republican ticket, because it means the defeat of the party." See the *Milwaukee Sentinel*, June 3, 1916.

[41] Roosevelt to Lodge, November 27, December 7, 1915, and February 4, 1916, in *Correspondence of Roosevelt and Lodge*, 2:464, 466–467, 479.

After the Chicago conference Roosevelt's attacks upon the German-Americans became more furious than ever. In a speech delivered at St. Louis the day after it concluded, which the editor of the *World* (who was rarely impressed by anything that Roosevelt said) called "hitting straight from the shoulder," he denounced the Alliance as an "anti-American Alliance" and its activities as "moral treason to the Republic." Its branches in different parts of the country were attempting "to coerce timid and unscrupulous politicians by threatening to vote against them" when their actions were "unsatisfactory from the standpoint, not of the United States, but of Germany." "These branches of the Alliance openly take the ground that they intend to shape American politics in the interests, not of the United States, but of Germany." The National Alliance, he also charged, with some injustice, had "put forth no program affecting America." [42]

On June 5 the Chicago Alliance, perhaps along with many others which failed to go on record, sent protests to the Republican National Convention against the possible nomination of Roosevelt and Root. Three days later Roosevelt returned to the attack, in the form of a long message to the Progressive National Convention. The "professional German-Americans," he warned that assembly, were endeavoring to terrorize the National Conventions in an attempt to secure the election of "a man who shall not be in good faith an American President, but the viceroy of a foreign government."

The professional German-Americans, acting through various agencies, including the so-called German-American Alliances, are at this moment serving notice on the members of your Convention that your action must be taken with a view to the interests, not of the United States, but of Germany and of that section of the German-American vote which is anti-American to the core. . . .

[42] *World*, June 1, 1916; *Milwaukee Sentinel,* June 1, 1916.

It is for your Convention, in emphatic fashion, to repudiate them.

Several weeks before the Republican National Convention there had been indications that many German-Americans would accept Charles Evans Hughes as their presidential candidate. In March, Alphonse G. Koelble had declared in an interview that the Supreme Court justice was the German-American choice, but had, however, been severely rebuked by *The Fatherland,* which still thought Hughes "an absolutely unknown quantity" who might be "under the same mental pro-British bias as Lodge, Eliot, Root, and Roosevelt." German-American clubs to promote the nomination of Hughes, as against Roosevelt, began to spring up in the East. On May 29 the Alliance of Elizabeth, New Jersey, indorsed him as "the right man for the position and one of high character who would be neutral in all matters." On June 6 H. A. Metz, Henry Weismann, and George Sylvester Viereck declared their readiness to give him their support. When the national convention met, there followed numerous other pledges in his favor.[43]

Hughes received the Republican nomination on June 10. Immediately the German-language newspapers began to warm up to his candidature; the *Milwaukee-Sonntagspost* of June 11 published a front-page picture of him and Mrs. Hughes as "the next president and his wife." On the following day a group of prominent German-American citizens in Pennsylvania launched an appeal on his behalf. On the thirteenth he was indorsed by the Teutonic Sons of America. According to a statement in the *World,* Ferdinand Walther,

[43] *Hearings on the German-American Alliance,* 100; *Times,* May 24, 30, June 7, 9, 1916; *Fatherland,* vol. 4, no. 8, p. 122 (March 29, 1916). It is interesting to note that, on October 30, 1906, Hexamer had reprimanded Richard Lohrmann, then president of the New York Alliance, for indorsing Hughes for governor—ostensibly because this was against the constitution of the Alliance, which forbade participation in party politics, but probably also because Hughes was suspected of favoring prohibition. *Hearings on the German-American Alliance,* 538.

president of the Chicago Alliance, set out to organize the German vote of the Middle West behind him.[44] In July, Julius Moersch, president of the Minnesota Alliance, who had been sent by Keller to Montana as an agitator against prohibition, was found to be spending most of his time canvassing for Hughes and denouncing Wilson.[45]

In the months which followed, the German-language newspapers watched Hughes' campaign with ever-increasing interest, and gave full report to all his speeches. At the various conventions of the Alliances his candidature was supported with considerable enthusiasm. When the Central Alliance of Pennsylvania met on August 6, it was joined by representatives of the Patriotic League of America, an organization to further the Republican cause. Its chairman, John B. Mayer, opened the convention with an attack on Wilson, and used his influence later in the debates to recommend the election of Hughes. The name of the justice was applauded at the convention of the Illinois Alliance on September 10 and 11. On September 24 the Allegheny County Alliance of Pennsylvania promised him its support, having originally, as we have seen, declared for Henry Ford. At the same time it issued leaflets to its members, urging them to stand united behind the Republican lead. On September 28 the California Alliance called upon "all those who did not want the United States to become once more a British colony" to vote for Hughes and defeat Wilson at any price. The Ohio Alliance, with equal ardor, followed with its indorsement on October 1.[46]

According to the varied panegyrics of German-American

[44] *Times,* June 13, 1916; *Milwaukee Sentinel,* June 14, 1916; *World,* June 14, 1916. "We have 2,000,000 votes," claimed Louis E. Brandt, secretary of the Chicago Alliance, "and then again the Irish are with us, especially since the revolt in Dublin and the Sinn Fein executions." *World,* June 14, 1916.

[45] Testimony of Jacob Kennedy before the Senate subcommittee, in *Brewing and Liquor Interests,* 2:2664.

[46] *Germania-Herold,* August 7, 1916; *New-Yorker Staats-Zeitung,* September 12, 29, 1916; *Hearings on the German-American Alliance,* 320–328; *Mitteilungen,* November, 1916, p. 3; *Westliche Post,* October 3, 1916.

orators, Hughes was at once "the Bismarck of America" and "the new Lincoln." Henry Weismann, who had by this time overcome his distrust of the Republican party leaders sufficiently to permit himself once more to enter the political limelight, lauded him as follows at a meeting on October 27: "I believe in Mr. Hughes and in his assurance of his love of peace. He will not be a power in the hands of the munition interests. Wall Street cannot control him, nor can Roosevelt, Root, or any other of the elements of Republicanism, to whose possible domination many men, otherwise hostile to Mr. Wilson's cause, may take exception." In Milwaukee a Lutheran pastor even made efforts to extol the cause of Hughes from his pulpit—to the sore annoyance of many of his congregation. In New York the Reverend G. C. Berkemeier, editor of the official German publication of the General Council of the Lutheran Church, came out editorially for Hughes, only to be subsequently rebuked for his ardor. At St. Louis the Missouri Alliance held a special executive meeting on October 29, at which, "after a comparison of the public activities of Woodrow Wilson with those of Charles Evans Hughes," it arrived at the conclusion that "all American citizens who have the full interest of the United States at heart should, without hesitation, vote for Charles Evans Hughes." This recommendation, together with a recital of all Wilson's sins against American neutrality, was circulated to branches throughout the state. On the eve of the election the same Alliance, through its affiliation with the American Independence Union, helped to distribute a hundred and fifty thousand leaflets in favor of the Republicans.[47]

For reasons already considered, the National Alliance was prevented from officially recommending the cause of any

[47] *Times*, October 28, November 8, 1916; *New-Yorker Staats-Zeitung*, October 31, 1916; *Westliche Post*, October 30, November 7, 1916. The clergyman referred to was pastor of the Immanuel Church. "Confusion and turmoil followed this announcement and many of the younger element of the congregation, about 30 out of 600, walked out as a protest against the introduction of politics into a church service." *Times*, October 31, 1916.

candidate. On September 30 it issued a circular in which it stated that the "Alliance as such pursues no political aims. As an institution chartered by Congress, it is not permitted to engage in politics or take part in the campaign in a manner which would correspond with the views of the overwhelming majority of the German-American electorate. That does not prevent its members, and those of its state Alliances which are not in possession of a charter, from taking a lively interest in politics."[48] In this manner it kept on the safe side of the law. Yet in the same circular it did urge upon the German-Americans the duty of taking part in the election.

The rest was left to Hexamer personally. On October 12 he drew up a memorandum, copies of which were sent to all branch officers and to Wilson himself. These were accompanied by letters on private stationery, stating that they were issued by him as an ordinary citizen and printed at his own personal expense, and urging that "the time has come when German-Americans must come out openly and fearlessly for Hughes and Fairbanks."[49] The main text of the memorandum read as follows:

No self-respecting American of German birth or extraction can vote for President Wilson. What, as American patriots, are we to do? It has been suggested by several of our newspapers that German-Americans should entirely refrain from voting at the next presidential election. Such a course would be childish and unpatriotic. We certainly, as men, cannot pout and sulk like punished children. It is the duty of every American citizen not only fearlessly to express his convictions, but it is also a sacred trust imposed upon him as a free American citizen that he should vote at every primary and regular election.

Others have suggested that we concentrate our vote on a certain

[48] *Milwaukee-Sonntagspost,* October 1, 1916.
[49] The letter is printed in *Hearings on the German-American Alliance,* 98. It is interesting to note that it bears the letterhead "E. Hexamer and Son, Civil Engineers and Insurance Surveyors," but Hexamer had officially retired from business at the beginning of May, 1915. *Milwaukee-Sonntagspost,* May 16, 1915.

minority party (which has not the slightest chance of winning). This practically means the throwing away of our votes.

After much anxious thought, I have therefore decided to cast my vote for Hughes and Fairbanks.[50]

Hexamer's words would carry as much weight when he spoke as a private citizen as when he spoke as president of the National Alliance. This was, as he himself said, the first time in sixteen years (that is, in the history of the Alliance) that he had ventured to recommend any person for public office. He had therefore broken what might be regarded as a tradition of the organization. According to *The Fatherland* of October 25, "great importance was attached to his statement," and his action was regarded as a "strong card for the Republicans." One effect, it was expected, would be to check the talk among certain German-Americans of voting for the Socialists in order to punish both the larger parties. The memorandum was published prominently in most of the German-language newspapers, many of them making it an occasion to intensify their campaign against Wilson.[51]

Meanwhile the conference committee appointed at Chicago on May 29 had diligently carried out the duties entrusted to it. It met in New York shortly after the conference and appointed a subcommittee to interview the Republican nominee. Before the interview took place, however, another acute problem arose to cause the German-Americans some concern. This came with the publication by the British government on July 18 of a blacklist of eighty-five American firms with which, because of the commercial relations of the latter with the Central Powers, British subjects were forbidden to trade. Many of these firms were of German-American ownership, and so the indignation felt in the United States as a whole was particularly strong among the German-

---

[50] *New-Yorker Staats-Zeitung,* October 14, 1916; *Milwaukee-Sonntagspost,* October 15, 1916.

[51] See, for example, the editorial, "Wilson als Tyrann," in *Volksblatt und Freiheits-Freund,* October 31, 1916.

Americans. Hence when the subcommittee interviewed Hughes, it was charged, above all, to sound him on his attitude toward the British blacklist.[52]

No record of the interview was ever published and it was kept a secret from the press. According to Mr. von Bosse, secretary of the conference committee, the interview was granted in New York City. Hughes was apparently unwilling to say anything in private which he had not already said in public. "Mr. Hughes was very non-committal, explaining that he was opposed to *all* blacklists, no matter from what source they came, and also to all blockades." This satisfied the German-Americans, since the blacklist and the blockade were the work of the Allies. "Mr. Hughes was not considered pro-German by the German-Americans, but he was acceptable as not being anti-German."[53]

On October 9 Hughes came out with a strong condemnation of the blacklist at Philadelphia, in a speech which was hailed with delight by the German-language press.[54] A week later the conference committee published its report, which was printed in all the German-language newspapers and was also issued in leaflet form. The report began with an answer to the claim of Wilson's supporters that "he kept us out of war." It was to "Secretary Bryan, the American Congress, and the German government," it retorted (somewhat unjustly, in view of Wilson's determination to keep out of war at the time of the *Lusitania* tragedy), that belongs "whatever credit may attach to the maintenance of peace." Wilson, it added, "on three different occasions seemed determined to drag us into the European war." It then proceeded to relate the sins of his administration. "Traditional American poli-

[52] Wilson was as indignant as anyone over the British blacklist, and even asked Congress for the power to employ retaliatory action. See *Munitions Industry*, 16–17, 52–54.
[53] Von Bosse to the writer, February 5, 1938. This is the first account of the interview to go on record.
[54] *Westliche Post*, October 10, 1916.

cies have been trodden under foot; our proud ideals igno-
miniously surrendered; a course of easy virtue to capture
votes is the only course which the administration has steered
consistently and persistently." To silence criticism of his
administration, it was charged, Wilson had "instructed the
government secret service to invoke methods which forcibly
recall Russia and the Cossack terror." The report then concluded with a strong indorsement of Hughes:

He is fair, firm, and a true American. We are confident that his
cabinet will be composed of real Americans, and not foreign sympathizers and agents of alien interests. We are confident also that
he will not be dominated by any clique of Wall Street or elsewhere. . . .

In Mr. Hughes' keeping the honor of our nation will be safe
— it will not be surrendered to the glamor of foreign influence or
the glitter of foreign gold. Every true American, every friend
of humanity, every advocate of fair play, every one, in fact, who
prays for the peace and prosperity of all nations, especially in the
fields of industry and commerce at home, may safely vote for
Charles E. Hughes.[55]

As the campaign of 1916 advanced, the Alliance thus became identified, if only unofficially, with the Republican
cause. With Wilson's renomination so definitely a foregone
conclusion, it had for the most part ignored the Democratic
Party leaders, although some of them, despite Wilson (and
perhaps because of him), were in sympathy with it on the
question of American neutrality. The support which it gave
to the Republicans was entirely unsolicited, yet not exactly
unacceptable. Hughes himself, in view of the large body of
anti-German feeling among the rest of his followers, was
somewhat shy to welcome it. He never acknowledged it publicly, nor, on the other hand, did he ever repudiate it. In a

[55] *Times,* October 21, 1916; *New-Yorker Staats-Zeitung,* October 17, 1916;
Germania-Herold, October 19, 1916. Leaflets F83614 DE. and F83614 NA., in
the Wisconsin State Historical Library.

way his German-American following tended to tie his hands at a difficult stage in his campaign. This may have been no real handicap, for the German-Americans may have had the strength and the solidarity to enable him to win in the end. But that would depend upon what Wilson could do in the meantime, and how the country as a whole would accept the German-American stand.

VII

WILSON'S REPUDIATION OF THE HYPHEN VOTE

In the election of 1916 both Wilson and the German-Americans charged that the other side was un-American. Yet it was perhaps a poor line of attack on the part of the German-Americans. To talk about the president's policy being un-American was, on the face of it, not very convincing. Somehow the country as a whole could not be persuaded that the course of neutrality which he had pursued was entirely to the detriment of the United States. As supreme head of the nation, with its destiny in his hands, he was obviously the one who stood in the most intimate relation to American interests. And in view of the fact that most of the German-American leaders had been so violently pro-German since the beginning of the war, it was hard for them to convince the general public (just or unjust as their case may have been), above the voice of the president, that they were the most unsullied representatives of true Americanism. Hence it was they who came to bear the stigma.

When they lent their support to Hughes, they tended to infect his candidature with some of the opprobrium that went with the hyphen. Although the preference of the German embassy was very definitely for Wilson (a fact, however, not widely known at the time),[1] Hughes began to find himself played up throughout the country as "the German candidate." Even during the Republican National Convention, Lucien Bonheur, the Long Island Progressive leader, had asked him for a statement on his German-American following,

---

[1] "I never for a moment denied that I personally would be glad to see Mr. Wilson re-elected, as I was convinced that he had the determination and the power to bring about peace." Bernstorff, *My Three Years in America*, 256.

adding that his failure to reply might lead him to "be considered the candidate of the German-American Alliance." It was also rumored that Roosevelt had expressed curiosity as to whether Hughes was to be the protégé of the Alliance.[2]

After his nomination the Democrats seized upon Hughes' German-American support as an opportunity to discredit his candidature.[3] The campaign *Text-Book* of the party stressed the fact that "agents of the German-American Alliance and other such organizations worked day and night in Chicago for him, promising German support if he were nominated."[4] The New York Democratic press tried to make it equally clear that his was the cause of Germany. Throughout July and August cartoons from the gifted pen of Rollin Kirby in the *World* depicted him before the shadow of the kaiser, or wearing a German helmet, or accompanied by the inevitable dachshund; and on each occasion the German-American Alliance managed to get into the picture by one means or another. An editorial by Frank Cobb on June 13, under the heading "Can the Kaiser defeat the President?" was representative of many similar, although perhaps less eloquent, attacks elsewhere. Officers of the Alliance, it was pointed out, had indorsed the Hughes nomination at Chicago even before the convention had finished its work. It had also received the immediate blessing of German propagandists like Viereck and Georg von Skal.

Whatever Mr. Hughes may say, whatever Mr. Hughes may do, he is the German candidate for President of the United States. He may not welcome this professional German-American support, but without it he could not have been nominated and without it he cannot be elected. . . .

[2] *Milwaukee Sentinel,* June 6, 1916; *World,* June 6, 1916.
[3] See, for example, the *Milwaukee Sentinel,* June 16, 1916. It is interesting to note that the French-language newspaper *Courrier des Etats-Unis* (published in New York) played up Hughes as the German candidate and Wilson as "the loyal candidate of the Allies." Quoted in an editorial in the *Westliche Post* (St. Louis), October 26, 1916.
[4] *Democratic Text-Book* (Democratic National Committee, New York and Chicago, 1916), 85.

If Mr. Hughes should be elected President his success would be regarded throughout the world as a tremendous victory for Germany in the United States. It would be a notice to all civilization that the German vote, and through the German vote the German Government, holds the balance of power in American politics. It would proclaim to the nations that no President of the United States could hereafter hope for re-election unless his foreign policy was satisfactory to Berlin and the Kaiser. It would make Potsdam the political capital of the United States, and in its moral effect upon Germany it would be more potent than a great victory of the German armies in the field.[5]

To such charges Hughes failed to make any really satisfactory reply. In the face of the many demands that he "set his heel upon the plan to carry an American election by votes based on a predominant loyalty to a foreign nation," he merely asserted vaguely that his attitude was "one of undiluted Americanism." "Anybody who supports me is supporting an out and out American and an out and out American policy and nothing else." When in a speech given on October 24 at Schützen Park, Long Island, he further declared, "I don't want the support of any one to whom the interest of this Nation is not supreme," he was loudly applauded by the German-Americans. This in itself was further evidence to the Democratic press that his "repudiations did not repudiate."[6]

Rumors began to circulate of a secret pact between Hughes and the German-Americans. On October 10 Norman Hapgood, editor of *Harper's Weekly,* charged that such an agreement had come into existence, and Senator Kent E. Keller of Illinois added that Victor Ridder of the *New-Yorker Staats-Zeitung* was even writing some of Hughes' speeches for him.[7]

[5] *World* (New York), June 13, 1916. See also the editorial, "We Fight mit Hughes," *ibid.,* June 15, 1916, and "The German Drive against Wilson," September 15, 1916.
[6] *Nation,* 103:389 (October 26, 1916) 389; statement to a reporter, in the *World,* June 14, 1915; *Times,* October 25, 26, 1915.
[7] *Times,* October 13, 1916. If that were the case, they were somewhat vague for so rabid a pro-German as Ridder.

At the same time it was said that St. John Gaffney, retiring United States consul from Munich, had brought money from Germany to be spent on the Republican cause.[8] Any comment in the press of Germany which seemed to approve of the German-American support of Hughes was seized upon by Democratic editors as proof of an understanding.[9] On October 23 the Democratic National Committee published the records of what was alleged to have been a secret meeting between the Republican candidate and a pro-German committee headed by Jeremiah O'Leary.[10]

The German-Americans had committed a political blunder in making it obvious at so early a date that they were irreconcilable to Wilson's re-election. In June, 1915, *The Fatherland,* embittered over the *Lusitania* controversy, had organized a straw vote among German-American newspaper editors. The result indicated that Wilson had "lost 92 per cent of the German-American vote."[11] It could thus be assumed that in any case the German-Americans would not be with him in 1916. It gave him and the party plenty of time to prepare for this eventuality. They could maneuver themselves, if necessary, into a position from which they could repudiate the German-American vote with advantage. In view of the subsequent campaign against the hyphen, it soon became, in the words of Ambassador Gerard, "an asset to have the German-Americans against him."[12]

[8] The rumor was, of course, vigorously denied. *Times,* October 12, 1916.
[9] See Lansing, *War Memoirs,* 160–161.
[10] The committee called itself the American Independence Conference. It interviewed Hughes on September 20 with a view to getting a statement from him after he had congratulated Roosevelt on a speech in which the latter had attacked the German-Americans. *New-Yorker Staats-Zeitung,* October 23, 1916; *Times,* October 23, 1916; Jeremiah O'Leary, *My Political Trial and Experiences* (Jefferson Publishing Co., New York, 1919), 38–43; Viereck, *Spreading Germs of Hate,* 247–248.
[11] *Fatherland* (New York), vol. 2, no. 20, pp. 6–7 (June 23, 1915). See also "German-Americans Desert Wilson," in the *Literary Digest,* 50:1521 (June 26, 1915).
[12] Seymour, *Intimate Papers of Colonel House,* 2:23. "Any noise on our part," Bartholdt wrote to Koelble on December 21, 1915, "will but solidify Wilson's support and strengthen him." *World,* March 7, 1916.

For every German-American threat against Wilson there had been an assurance from his own followers that the loss of the German vote was anyway of no consequence. In October, 1915, George Harvey, in his usual vigorous and forthright manner, had used census statistics to demonstrate in the *North American Review* that the Germans could be outvoted by the elements from the Allied countries. "The German vote on a domestic topic," he added, "might be of great importance. The German vote on an alien topic, aiming to drag foreign influences and issues into American politics, would be a negligible quantity." Colonel House was likewise in no way dismayed by the German-American opposition. In discussing the election with Bernstorff on October 3, 1916, he expressed confidence of victory, despite the German-Americans, and assured the ambassador that "their votes against the President gave us no concern."[13]

Wilson made it his policy throughout the campaign openly to repudiate the vote of the German-Americans. He made no effort to answer the charges they raised against him, but used every opportunity publicly to express his contempt and distrust. There was perhaps considerable truth in the statement of the Milwaukee *Germania-Herold* of October 5 that he was "capitalizing on the hyphen."[14] He undoubtedly felt it to be his duty to take the stand he did, and perhaps honestly believed that the United States was being grievously wronged by the activities of the German-American groups. Yet the fact remains that his attitude was good politics, and that he suffered no permanent loss of votes by proclaiming himself the champion of an undivided national allegiance.[15]

Wilson's first public repudiation of the German-Americans

[13] *North American Review*, 202:502–504 (October, 1915); Seymour, *Intimate Papers of Colonel House*, 2:372.

[14] Editorial in the *Germania-Herold* (Milwaukee), October 5, 1916.

[15] "The loyalty maneuver was probably sincere, but it was certainly shrewd politics, for on election day it left the Administration secure in its attitude of patriotism, while putting Hughes on the defensive." Frederic L. Paxson, *Pre-War Years, 1913–1917* (Houghton Mifflin, Boston, 1936), 351.

was at the Democratic National Convention at St. Louis. It had been expected that the hyphen question would figure in some way in the platforms of both parties. At the Republican Convention Chairman Warren G. Harding had dealt with it somewhat soothingly in his opening address of June 7. "One must be human," he declared; "to be an American, he must have human sympathies and human loves; and I should pity the foreign-born and sons of foreign-born whose very souls are not wrung by the cataclysmal sorrow of the old world." When the party drew up its platform it devoted a paragraph to a stand for national unity and loyalty.[16]

The Democrats were to grapple more forcefully with the problem. In Wisconsin there had been a particularly lively feud between the Democratic leaders and the German-American Alliance. At the state convention of the party at Green Bay, Patrick Martin had attacked the aims and purpose of the latter as "high treason." Certain newspaper men in the state were also apparently willing to support the Democrats only on condition that their National Convention took a strong stand on the hyphen question. Hence on June 13 Senator Husting, whose election in 1914 had, ironically enough, been approved by the Wisconsin Alliance, hurled what the press described as a "bombshell" into the convention by demanding that it draw up a plank "to accept the challenge of the German-American Alliance." In his opinion the convention should create a specific issue to see if the German-Americans were really following the lead of the Alliance. "I do not believe that the German-Americans are being led by this movement, and I believe that they would welcome an opportunity to assert in a very positive manner their good Americanism."[17]

On the same day Tumulty, who invariably counseled a

[16] *Republican Campaign Text-Book* (Republican National Committee), 1916, p. 28; *Milwaukee Sentinel,* June 9, 1916.
[17] *Milwaukee-Sonntagspost,* July 23, 1916; *Germania-Herold,* August 25, 1914; *Milwaukee Sentinel,* June 14, 1915.

defiant stand against the German-Americans, wrote to Wilson urging him to use his influence for a plank such as Husting suggested. Pointing to the support which the Alliance was giving to Hughes, he argued that "we ought to meet these things in a manly, aggressive, and militant fashion." In response Wilson telegraphed Secretary of War Baker, his representative at the convention, to insist upon a "definite and unequivocal repudiation of the hyphen vote." On June 14 a tentative anti-hyphen plank was submitted. The convention, however, was not unanimous in its favor, and on June 15 some of the delegates began to work for a more mildly worded reply to the German-Americans. Yet Wilson refused to be moved from the stand he had taken, and was prepared to ask the convention to prolong its session so that he could go to St. Louis and make a personal appeal. It was even rumored that he would decline the nomination rather than have the plank changed.[18]

In the end Wilson's view prevailed. The Democratic Party platform, adopted on June 16, dealt at length with the hyphen issue. Professing serious concern over the question of divided allegiance, it made its appeal for Americanism much more specific than did the Republican. "In this day of test," it declared, "America must show itself, not a nation of partisans, but a nation of patriots"; and then called upon "all men of whatever origin or creed, who would count themselves Americans to join in making clear to all the world their unity and consequent power of America." It denounced the "racial strife" which proceeded from the efforts of those "actuated by the purpose to promote the interest of a foreign power in disregard of our own country's welfare." Then in the following terms it singled out the German-American Alliance and similar organizations for special condemnation:

We condemn all alliances and combinations of individuals in this country, of whatever nationality or descent, who agree and

---

[18] Tumulty, *Woodrow Wilson as I Know Him,* 188–191; Sullivan, *Our Times,* 5:236–237; *Milwaukee Sentinel,* June 15, 16, 1916.

conspire together for the purpose of embarrassing or weakening our Government or of improperly influencing or coercing our public representatives in dealing or in negotiating with any foreign powers. We charge that such conspiracies among a limited number exist and have been instigated for the purpose of advancing the interests of foreign countries to the prejudice and detriment of our country. We condemn any political party which, in view of the activity of such conspirators, surrenders its integrity or modifies its policy.[19]

As a result of this stand many German-American Democrats began to desert the party. Returning from a tour of the East on October 1, Bartholdt reported that he found the German-American Democrats there more bitterly opposed to Wilson than the Republicans. Alphonse G. Koelble of the New York German Societies had been for a long time chairman of the Manhattan Borough committee of the party and one of the secretaries of the general committee of Tammany Hall. On October 4 he resigned both offices, declaring that "I am quitting because I cannot retain my connection with an organization that is working for the re-election of President Wilson." In other parts of the country, especially in Ohio, where the German-American Democrats were numerous, there were reports of wholesale defections from the party. Of all the German-language newspapers in the country, only the *Staats-Anzeiger* of Bismarck, North Dakota, showed any inclination to favor the Democratic cause.[20]

Despite Wilson, there were a few frantic efforts by certain Democratic politicians to retain the German vote. On July 18 Charles Lieb of Indiana, himself of German birth, pleaded for Wilson in the House of Representatives.[21] According to

[19] *Milwaukee Sentinel*, June 17, 1916.

[20] *New York Times*, October 1, 21, 1916; *World*, October 5, 1916; *New-Yorker Staats-Zeitung*, November 6, 1916. Three German-language papers, the Chicago *Abendpost*, the *Milwaukee Demokrat*, and the Buffalo *Demokrat*, were against Hughes, but not for Wilson. *New York Times*, October 1, 1916.

[21] *Congressional Record*, 64 Congress, 1 Session, 53:11254–11258. Lieb also quoted a telegram to Wilson from General Frederick C. Winkler of Milwaukee, who had fought with Schurz in the Civil War and who had been as-

Viereck, the National Committee of the party offered to buy a million copies of *The Fatherland* if it would print an article by James K. McGuire which asked certain embarrassing questions of Hughes. Senator Stone, always very strongly attached in sympathy to the German side, denounced Hughes in a speech at Terrace Garden, New York, on September 16, as an "anti-German Welshman." Stone also persuaded Victor Ridder and Viereck to discuss with him the attitude of the German-Americans toward Wilson. Postmaster Burleson entered into a similar conference, but no tangible result came of either meeting.[22] Attempts were made to differentiate between the *kaiserliche* Germans and the Forty-Eighters, in an appeal to those who cherished the democratic traditions of the latter.[23] The Democratic State Committee of Wisconsin appealed for German speakers to take part in the campaign, and the National Committee even set up a "German Division" to issue pamphlets in the German language. One of these endeavored to persuade the German-Americans to spurn the lead of the Alliance and not let "German sympathies and feelings, or their injured pride, be projected as a national issue into the campaign."[24]

Wilson, however, remained obdurate in his determination to repudiate the German vote. On June 14 he devoted the main part of his Flag Day address at Washington to the alleged disloyalty of certain elements. "A new sort of division of feeling," he said, had "sprung up among us." Many of the

sociated with the Wisconsin Alliance in its pro-German activities. See the *Milwaukee Free Press*, August 19, 1914. "A Republican voter since 1860, I hold that in the present crisis the party has no place. True Americanism must stand by the man who stands manfully at the helm. I support your re-election." *Milwaukee Free Press*, July 4, 1916.

[22] Viereck, *The Strangest Friendship in History*, 159; *New York Times*, October 11, 12, 13, 1916; *World*, October 13, 1916. See also the editorial, "Nur für die Öffentlichkeit bestimmt!" in the *New Yorker Volkszeitung*, October 13, 1916.

[23] See, for example, the letter of Frank Bohn in the *New York Times*, October 26, 1916.

[24] *Germania-Herold*, September 29, 1916; *Westliche Post*, October 30, 1916; pamphlet, *Hughes oder Wilson*, quoted in the *New-Yorker Staats-Zeitung*, October 24, 1916.

foreign-born, he believed, were "as loyal to the flag of the
United States as any native citizen," but "there is disloyalty
active in the United States, and it must be absolutely crushed.
It proceeds from a minority, but a very active and subtle minority. It works underground, but it shows its ugly head where
we can see it; and there are those at this moment who are
trying to levy a species of political blackmail, saying 'Do what
we wish in the interest of foreign sentiment or we will wreak
our vengeance at the polls.'"[25] On July 13, before a convention on Americanization, he made what was taken to be an attack on the Chicago conference of May 28 and 29. Certain
men—"I never believed a great number"—he declared, who
had been "born in foreign lands" had given the government
concern by preferring the interests of those lands to the interests of the United States. "They have even gone so far as to
draw apart in spirit and in organization from the rest of us to
accomplish some special object of their own."[26]

In accepting the Democratic nomination at Shadow Lawn
on September 2 the president, prompted a little by Tumulty,
returned again to the hyphen question. "The passions and intrigues," he said, "of certain active groups and combinations
of men amongst us who were born under foreign flags injected
the poison of disloyalty into our most critical affairs." It was
part of the business of "this year of reckoning" to deal with
the disloyalty of these groups. For himself, he emphatically
repudiated the votes of any such persons. "I am the candidate
of a party," he said, "but I am above all things an American
citizen. I neither seek the favor nor fear the displeasure of that
small alien element which puts loyalty to any foreign power
before loyalty to the United States."[27] When, on September

[25] New York Times, June 15, 1916. See also the editorial, "The Disloyalists,"
June 16, 1916; Milwaukee Sentinel, June 15, 1916; Baker and Dodd, Public
Papers of Woodrow Wilson, 2:209; Democratic Text-Book, 1916, pp. 79–92.
[26] New York Times, July 14, 1916; Baker and Dodd, Public Papers of Woodrow Wilson, 2:251.
[27] Tumulty, Woodrow Wilson, 208–209; New York Times, September 3, 1916;
Baker and Dodd, Public Papers of Woodrow Wilson, 2:282–283.

29, Jeremiah O'Leary sent him a telegram reprimanding him for his "truckling to the British Empire" and his "dictatorship over Congress," Wilson replied: "I would feel deeply mortified to have you or anybody like you vote for me. Since you have access to many disloyal Americans, and I have not, I will ask you to convey this message to them."[28]

O'Leary's telegram was really so abusive that it made many German-Americans shudder, and even the German-language press, despite its bitterness toward Wilson, commented adversely upon it. But the use that the president made of it to issue a peremptory and final repudiation of the hyphen vote was the political master stroke of the campaign. His reply was given before a special conference of newspaper men, and was received with loud applause by the Democratic press. In the opinion of Tumulty, it won the hearty and unanimous approval of the country for the president. According to Lansing, it was a piece of political strategy that could hardly be matched in any presidential campaign. "It made thousands of votes for its author." One Democratic National Committee man, quoted in the *New York Tribune,* declared that it "nailed Hughes' effort to win the German vote to a flagpole," where all could see it. The Democrats, he added, were "going to make the hyphen issue the big talking point of this campaign. There isn't any other issue."[29]

Thus the hyphen question contributed to Wilson's re-election to an extent not generally recognized. It would of course be absurd to ascribe his success to any one cause. When the issue of an election is to be decided by the casting of so many millions of votes, representing such widely diverse interests, as in the United States, the outcome necessarily depends upon a multitude of complex factors and causes. Not one of these

[28] *Literary Digest,* 53:935 (October 14, 1916); O'Leary, *My Political Trial and Experiences,* 45–47.
[29] *Germania-Herold,* September 30, 1916; Tumulty, *Woodrow Wilson,* 214; Lansing, *War Memoirs,* 162–163; *Literary Digest,* 53:935 (October 14, 1916), quoting, with other comments, the item from the *New York Tribune.*

can be entirely isolated from the rest. But we cannot lose slight of the fact that, for the very reason that all the pro-German leaders were so vociferously for Hughes, many of those who were pro-Ally, and many more who were just plainly pro-American, would be likely to cast their votes for Wilson. Hence there was probably considerable truth in a *New York Times* editorial of October 2 which professed to see symptoms of "an aroused Americanism." "The German vote is a myth, and where not a myth it is a minority as against the votes of outraged men who put this country first." And in another editorial of November 9, just after the election: "A survey of the returns by states fails to disclose where the hyphenate vote threw a single electoral vote to Hughes. Either there was no hyphen vote or it was cancelled or more than cancelled in its own territory by anti-hyphen votes."[30]

Hughes' German-American support was the support of a minority—and of a minority which in its views on foreign policy was utterly irreconcilable with the majority support that he was receiving from other sources. By one of the strange ironies of the campaign both Theodore Roosevelt and the German-American Alliance were working assiduously for the Republican candidate. Yet the one was the very antithesis of the other. As a result there was complete lack of harmony and coordination among Hughes' following. In many of the speeches in which he commended the cause of Hughes, Roosevelt renewed his attacks upon the German-Americans. When on October 26 certain Republican leaders in Chicago asked him to "soft-pedal" the hyphen question, he threatened to retire from the campaign rather than comply. His attitude really played directly into the hands of Wilson, who had already declared himself unwilling to be supported by the element he was so persistent in attacking. "If Mr. Hughes is defeated," wrote Viereck in *The Fatherland*, "he owes his defeat to the Colonel." Hence it is perhaps not surprising that

[30] *New York Times,* October 2, November 9, 1916.

Wilson carried such large German-American centers as St. Louis and Milwaukee, and that in Cincinnati Hughes suffered a considerable slump in the normal Republican plurality.[31]

The actual numerical strength which would accrue to Hughes as a result of the open support of the Alliance was probably very small. It was not that he could count upon the votes of the two million members of the Alliance over and above what he would otherwise have received. For the larger portion of the German-Americans were Republicans in any case, and would, without any lead from the Alliance, have been almost sure to vote according to their party affiliation. This fact is substantiated by a political survey taken by the *World* at the beginning of July. Bearing in mind this newspaper's avowedly Democratic bias, we still see that in most of the states where they were numerically important, the German-Americans tended to be overwhelmingly Republican. Thus in California they were seventy per cent Republican; in Missouri, seventy-five per cent Republican; and in Illinois, seventy per cent Republican.[32] When they favored the Demo-

---

[31] *Ibid.*, October 27, 1916; *Fatherland*, vol. 5, no. 15, p. 234 (November 15, 1916). See the comments of prominent German-Americans on the election in the *World*, November 11, 1916. According to Mr. J. Otto Pfeiffer, editor of the *Westliche Post*, it is hard to say whether, in the end, the German-American support which had been promised to Hughes materialized or not. Certainly the German-Americans did not follow entirely the lead given by their newspapers, for Hughes tended to be as vague as Wilson was adamant on issues which were vital in the eyes of the German-Americans. Mr. Pfeiffer himself, then assistant editor of *Amerika* (St. Louis), took the attitude that the German-Americans should vote only for congressmen and make these exert pressure on the president. Conversation with the writer, St. Louis, December 28, 1937. Somewhat similar views are expressed in the *New Yorker Volkszeitung*, November 13, 1916. The slogan "He kept us out of war" undoubtedly opened the eyes of some German-Americans to the fact that it was perhaps Wilson, after all, who had kept the country at peace.

Mr. Siegmund G. von Bosse adds the following comment to this chapter: "Much of the German-American vote was thrown to Wilson on account of his known anti-Prohibition attitude; indeed the brewers gave it out that he was their candidate for this reason."

[32] In Wisconsin, where the German-Americans numbered 40 per cent of the voters, 40 per cent were normally Republicans and 60 per cent Democrats, but many of the latter were expected to support Hughes. In Colorado, where the German-Americans constituted 15 per cent of the whole voting power, 60 per cent were Republicans. In Iowa and Indiana prohibition complicated the

crats, it was often because the Republicans tended toward prohibition, and even in this case, when prohibition was not at the time an issue, they might vote Republican in a national election.

In some few cases, members of the Alliance who were Democrats refused to follow the official lead in favor of Hughes. The Texas Alliance as a whole remained loyal to the Democratic Party.[33] There was some trouble in Ohio. On October 30 the Canton Alliance, with its three hundred members, withdrew from the state Alliance rather than support the Republican candidate. The Gallion Alliance had already withdrawn for the same reason, and there were also defections in Toledo.[34]

It has even been suggested that the opinions of Ambassador Bernstorff may have played some part in the election. He was very definitely in favor of Wilson. He discussed the progress of the campaign with House. He even begged Viereck to stop the vitriolic attacks upon Wilson in *The Fatherland*.[35] According to Viereck, "his word may have been the grain that tipped the scale against Hughes."[36] Yet the preferences of Bernstorff were never made widely public. And in so far as the German-Americans seem to have been constantly at variance with the German embassy on other questions, there is little reason to believe that they were disposed to fall in line on this, a question, presumably, of domestic politics.

In thus following the campaigns of 1916 from the standpoint of the German-American vote, and especially from the standpoint of the German-American Alliance, it has been possible to stress the part played by the sympathies and preju-

party issue because the Republicans were being supported by the Anti-Saloon League. See the political survey in the *World*, July 1, 2, 1916.

[33] Testimony of Paul Meerscheidt in *Hearings on the German-American Alliance*, 189.

[34] *New York Times*, October 31, 1916.

[35] Partly, however, because they embarrassed his relations with the Department of State. Viereck, *The Strangest Friendship in History*, 159–160.

[36] *Ibid.*, 160. See also Lansing, *War Memoirs*, 164.

dices aroused by the European war. So deeply colored was the election by the issues of that war that one might be tempted to regard it as the culmination of the long struggle between the forces of Ally and Teuton in the United States. Some historian of the future might indeed describe it, not entirely inaccurately, as "the European war in America." For in no other American election—not even in the boisterous days of the Know-Nothing movement—were the lines of racial cleavage quite so apparent. In no other election, at least not since the French interference in the election of 1796, were votes so readily determined by the stand which people had taken toward one side or the other in a foreign crisis in which the United States itself was, after all, not directly concerned.

VIII

DECLINE AND FALL OF
·THE ALLIANCE

To a large extent the defeat of Hughes was the defeat of the Alliance. Into the election, which might be regarded as the climax of all its activities, both locally and nationally, it had thrown its entire strength and every effort.[1] It came out somewhat broken. It was forced to contemplate another four years of office of a president whom it had done its utmost to defeat, and whom a report in its bulletin of December, 1916, referred to with some dread (although rather unjustly, for Wilson was never so vindictive) as a *Deutschenfresser*. As we have seen, the Democratic Party platform had condemned this and all other such alliances of foreign-born citizens. In the letter of October 12, 1916, accompanying his declaration for Hughes, Hexamer had significantly warned his fellow officials that "if Wilson is elected . . . we shall be made powerless for a long time."[2] Comment in the press after the election seemed to bear out very strongly the truth of this prediction. A contributor to *World's Work* of December, 1916, wrote that the election had "closed one chapter in American history" in a way that reflected the utmost credit upon the American spirit and American institutions. "The phantom of German-Americanism, which has been haunting the United States for the last two years, has definitely been laid." According to the *World,* which had perhaps given it more adverse publicity than any other newspaper, the hyphen had been "put out of business in this country." "For some time to come, no doubt, we shall hear from the inner circles of

[1] "Die Präsidentenwahl hat als Probiertigel gedient." Siegmund G. von Bosse, "Einiges Deutschamerikanertum: Traum oder Wirklichkeit," in *Mitteilungen,* April, 1917, p. 2.
[2] *Ibid.,* December, 1916, p. 5; *Hearings on the German-American Alliance,* 98.

transplanted Prussianism strange boasts of the wonderful accomplishments of German discipline in the United States, but they will be only the dubious thanksgivings and apologies of misguided men for the few crumbs which they have picked up under the great table of Americanism."[3]

There was, however, another factor which added to the difficulties of the Alliance in the succeeding months. This was the ever deepening commitment of the United States, financially and industrially, to the Allied cause. So great had this become that on October 23, 1916, the secretary of commerce, reporting upon the possibility of retaliatory legislation against the British blacklist, advised against its use because it would prove as injurious to American as to Allied trade. The first Allied loan, which the Alliance had so strenuously opposed, was floated in October, 1915, at a half billion dollars. On August 1, 1916, France obtained a loan for one hundred million dollars and on September 1 Great Britain a loan for two hundred and fifty million. In October Great Britain obtained another three hundred million, and in February, 1917, another two hundred and fifty million. At the same time relations with Germany remained, in many respects, as strained as ever. The threat of another submarine crisis had not been dispelled, for in its note of May 14, 1916, accepting American conditions on the question, the German government had pointed out that if the United States failed to force Great Britain to observe international law, it would be compelled to use once more this highly controversial method of warfare.[4]

The Alliance had not given up entirely the idea of hampering what it considered to be an unneutral and one-sided trade. Many branches began to agitate for an embargo on foodstuffs, claiming that the ever increasing exports to Allied countries were driving up the cost of living in the United States. This was the argument advanced by the Central Alli-

[3] *World's Work*, 33:117 (December, 1916); *World*, November 10, 1916.
[4] *Munitions Industry*, 16–17.

ance of Pennsylvania at its annual convention at Erie on
August 6, 1916.[5] On January 2, 1917, the Allegheny County
Alliance dealt with the question at some length, and drew
up the following resolutions to be sent to members of Congress and of the General Assembly of Pennsylvania:

Resolved That we most earnestly condemn that course of action
which brings need to the citizens of America, while it favors
foreign peoples, thereby bringing the principle "America First"
to naught;

Resolved That we voice an insistent and especially urgent demand to command a stop to such unheard-of conditions and to
place an embargo on the export of all grains and food products.[6]

On December 12 the German government issued its abor-
tive note, glorying in the resistance and confidence of the
Central Powers, but expressing a readiness "to stem the flow
of blood and bring the horrors of war to an end." A week
later Wilson invited both sets of belligerents to state their
war aims and their views "as to the terms which must precede
those ultimate arrangements for the peace of the world."
Once more peace became a topic of wide discussion among the
leaders of the Alliance. By many Wilson's efforts at mediation
met with a hearty welcome. But by some they were greeted
with suspicion. To a certain extent the whole idea of Germany making overtures for peace at this stage was difficult
to reconcile with the reports in the German-language newspapers, which, with glaring headlines, had talked only of
German victories since August, 1914. Hence Leo Stern, in an
interview as president of the Wisconsin Alliance, declared
himself firmly opposed to all peace-at-any-price movements—
"because I don't want to see Germany and her allies robbed
of the fruits of their hard-fought victory." Likewise John B.
Mayer, at a meeting of the Philadelphia Alliance on January
4, welcomed the thought of "a wholesome peace for the old

[5] *New-Yorker Staats-Zeitung*, August 7, 1916.
[6] *Hearings on the German-American Alliance*, 324–325.

fatherland," but hoped that it would be brought about with England on her knees.[7]

The situation, already far from pleasant, became extremely critical for the German-Americans on January 31, when Germany announced the resumption of unrestricted submarine warfare, and the United States replied by severing diplomatic relations. There was at once something of a panic in certain circles. Banks found themselves faced with a run of nervous German-American depositors. "Leave your money in the banks," the *New-Yorker Staats-Zeitung* had to urge its readers. "Be calm. Whatever may happen, citizen or non-citizen, your money is safe, and no American government, least of all the present, would think of touching it." In some cities there was an unusually large rush of applications for citizenship papers. In Chicago ninety per cent of these were found to be from Germans and Austro-Hungarians.[8]

The task of the moment was to prevent the international crisis from developing into war. On February 5 the German-American Chamber of Commerce of New York issued a manifesto in which it argued that "he is the most loyal citizen who up to the last minute strives for peace with all his strength." On the following day Hexamer telegraphed all state presidents of the Alliance to "arrange peace meetings, adopting resolutions requesting Congress to submit the question of declaring war to a referendum, and send the resolutions to members of Congress by wire and letter." When his stand with reference to war became the object of considerable adverse comment, he issued to the press a statement of loyalty for the Alliance and for himself. The Alliance, he asserted, was "a law-abiding, peaceful institution." It contained nothing that was in contradiction to the interests of the United States. But on the war his views were those of William Jennings Bryan: had the common people of the countries now at

[7] *Munitions Industry,* 17; Paxson, *Pre-War Years,* 367 ff., 377 ff.; *Milwaukee-Sonntagspost,* January 7, 1917.
[8] *New-Yorker Staats-Zeitung,* February 6, 1917.

war had any voice in the matter, there would have been no war. "I consider it best," he concluded, "that people get together in a peaceful manner and draw up resolutions demanding from Congress a referendum to decide the question of war or peace."[9]

On February 7, in great haste, Hexamer summoned to Philadelphia officials of the Alliance from twenty-eight states. The meeting, which lasted until midnight, dealt almost exclusively with the diplomatic rupture between the United States and Germany. It was held behind closed doors, but Hexamer later communicated the results to the press. It indorsed Wilson's actions in handing Bernstorff his passport and in recalling Gerard, and drew up a pledge of loyalty. "Under President Wilson, as our commander-in-chief," it promised, "we will fight no less loyally than the German-Americans fought under Lincoln in the Civil War for the preservation of the Union." In the event of war, provision was to be made for the enlistment of German-American regiments, presumably on the Civil War pattern, and any money that remained from German war relief work was to be given to the Red Cross. Then, with the following statement, the meeting concluded: "Our representatives understand that, since the beginning of the war, we have been very much misunderstood and unjustly criticized. But if it comes to war with Germany our attitude will permit no further misinterpretation, for we shall come forward with our fortunes and our lives for our American government."[10]

The decisions of this meeting created something of a sensation. In some German-American circles they were interpreted to mean that Hexamer had promised to deliver regiments of soldiers to the government in the event of war. A

[9] *Germania-Herold* (Milwaukee), February 7, 8, 1917; *New-Yorker Staats-Zeitung*, February 7, 1917; *Hearings on the German-American Alliance*, 193; *New York Times*, February 7, 1917.

[10] *Germania-Herold*, February 8, 1917; *New-Yorker Staats-Zeitung*, February 9, 1917.

few attempts were made to explain away the significance of the meeting. One explanation was that it had represented not the executive committee of the Alliance but merely those officers who were interested in German war relief work. On February 12 Hexamer stated that in any case he would vouchsafe for the loyalty of all members of the Alliance, for only American citizens had been admitted to its ranks.[11]

Unrest, however, continued, and culminated on March 1 in a fierce attack upon the officers of the Alliance by Christian Rebhan, president of the German War Veterans of New York. Rebhan denounced "those German-Americans who, for purely personal reasons, use every opportunity to enter the limelight and in gushing phrases proclaim their loyalty." He expressed resentment that such persons should profess to "speak for thousands, and even millions, of German-Americans." It was not true that the latter envisaged with equanimity the outbreak of war with Germany: "the bare thought of war fills us with deepest sorrow." "As long as there is the remotest possibility of avoiding war, it is our most sacred duty to concentrate upon it instead of making ourselves the accomplices of the war mongers." Rebhan also declared that the majority of the German-Americans did not approve the diversion to other purposes of money collected for the widows and orphans of German soldiers.[12]

The meeting of February 7 only expressed in a pointed manner what became the general policy of the Alliance: to make it clear that in the event of war it would show no hesitation in standing loyally by the United States. On February 10 the *New York Times* published a statement from Hexamer to the effect that "the National German-American Alliance must in this crisis stand on the same high plane of absolutely American patriotism which it has always upheld, and unless it does so it has no right to exist in our country." Six days

[11] *New-Yorker Staats-Zeitung,* February 13, 1917.
[12] *Milwaukee-Sonntagspost,* March 4, 1917.

later Colonel House received a visit from Bernard Ridder of the *New-Yorker Staats-Zeitung,* who came to tell him of the loyalty of the German-Americans. He outlined a plan for enlisting them to work on "committees of safety" in New York City, and left the colonel very favorably impressed. "I congratulated him," the latter recorded in his diary, "on the patriotism of the German-Americans and did what I could to stimulate that feeling." [13]

At the same time the branches of the Alliance bent every effort to keep the country at peace. On February 12 the American Independence Union at San Francisco, to which the local Alliance was affiliated, reminded Wilson by telegram that he had been re-elected because of his ability to keep the country out of war. The drift toward war was blamed on the financial magnates who had lent their money to the Allies. Senator Wesley L. Jones was so impressed by one statement of the German-American position that, "in justice to many of our citizens whose loyalty is repeatedly questioned," he had it inserted into the *Congressional Record* on February 14. This was a letter from H. Mahncke, president of the Washington Alliance, to all the German-Americans in the state, which read as follows:

Let us . . . defend our homes and our adopted land and all its institutions against Germany, if need be, as well as against any other nation or combination of nations which would dare to trample on our sacred rights. . . .

But then . . . as long as this country is not at war we have the right to enter a protest against what we consider unjust and unfair.

While we stand as one man for our country when it is in danger, we are not willing to offer ourselves and give over our sons for the benefit of any European nation. Nor are we willing

---

[13] *New York Times,* February 10, 1917; Seymour, *Intimate Papers of Colonel House,* 2:444. House says that it was Herman Ridder who came to see him, but it must have been Bernard Herman Ridder, son of the great Herman Ridder. Herman Ridder had died on November 1, 1916.

to sacrifice ourselves and our blood for Wall Street or any other combination of ammunition makers who might lose their fortunes if we do not uphold the hands of their creditors.[14]

On February 24 the Rochester Alliance of New York joined the Socialists in demonstrating against the possible entry of the United States into a war of foreign capitalists. According to a Declaration of Principles issued on March 12, the Reading branch of the Central Alliance of Pennsylvania, despite its "unconditional loyalty," felt itself driven to protest against the "treasonable agitation of certain agents" of the Allied Powers, which aimed at "dragging our country, at all costs, into the war." The entry of the United States into the war would have "no other purpose than to impose upon America the burden of the European war of nations," which a bankrupt Europe could not shoulder. "We believe that the majority of the inhabitants of our country, if informed of all the actual facts, would agree with us on all points and would raise a protest against war with Germany."[15]

From Wisconsin, as a result, to a great extent, of the stand taken by Senator La Follette, there came the most insistent German-American demand for the preservation of peace. At an executive meeting of the Milwaukee Alliance on February 12 it was urged that all members send individual appeals to Wilson to keep the country out of war. On March 16 the same branch, on behalf of its ten thousand members in the city, sent La Follette, who had hitherto not received very much attention from the Alliance, a telegram congratulating him on his "patriotic, manly, and fearless efforts" to keep the United States at peace. A motion of censure against the senator lay at the time before the Wisconsin legislature. Thus the Milwaukee Alliance also utilized the occasion to inform the members of that body from the city that it would expect

<hr />

[14] *Germania-Herold*, February 19, 1917; *Congressional Record*, 64 Congress, 2 Session, 54:3251.
[15] *New-Yorker Staats-Zeitung*, February 24, 1917; *Mitteilungen*, April, 1917, p. 3.

them to support no such proceedings. In Milwaukee itself
there was initiated an unofficial referendum on the war. Cards
asking the people to decide between war and peace, and to
send their answers to the two United States senators for
Wisconsin, were circulated in large quantities. The results
were said to have shown a vote of three hundred to one against
war.

After the declaration of war on April 6 the main anxiety of
the National Alliance was to preserve an attitude of absolute
correctness among the German-Americans. It continually
preached loyalty and enjoined a proper, law-abiding conduct.
"Everything must be avoided which is not in accordance with
the highest duty of a citizen of this country," urged the April
issue of *Mitteilungen*. "No German-American will forget the
duty which he owes the country of his choice, the country to
which he has given his best, and he will unite his utterances
and his deeds only with its best interests." The members of
the Alliance were warned against "alien agents who seek to
cast suspicion upon our loyalty," and were advised that "in
most cases it is better to say nothing and to believe very little
that others are reported to have said." On the very day that
war was declared, Henry Weismann called a special executive
meeting of the New York Alliance to take "immediate, intelligent, and urgent action" to demonstrate the loyalty of its
members. "The future of our standing," he declared, "in
this, our beloved country, depends largely upon the manner
in which we approach the great crisis. Of our loyalty there can
be no question."[16]

The state of war meant many great problems for the
country as a whole. It meant even greater problems for the
Alliance, which for nearly three years had vigorously cham-
pioned the cause of what was now the enemy. The May number of *Mitteilungen,* the first to be published after the United

[16] *Germania-Herold,* February 13, March 17, 31, April 4, 1917; *Milwaukee-
Sonntagspost,* March 11, 1917; *Mitteilungen,* April, 1917, pp. 4-5; *New York
Times,* April 7, 1917.

States entered the war, contained an editorial entitled "Peace and Patience," in which it was declared:

The annals of the history of our country teach us that, and with golden letters it will have to be written in the future history of this country: The American of German descent remained, in the most difficult time of trial that can be imagined, faithful to the oath to his adopted country, in unflinching and truly Germanic manner. Even though with bleeding heart, he has nevertheless himself fulfilled his duty toward his adopted fatherland uprightly and honestly in the war against his own mother country.

The same issue contained further exhortations to lawful conduct. Every obligation imposed by the war upon the members of the Alliance was to be conscientiously fulfilled. The right of meeting was not denied to the various branches, but they were to refrain from using the decorations which had hitherto been characteristic of such occasions—German flags and pictures of the kaiser. Some form of assistance was asked for those German-Americans who lost their livelihood as a result of war-time prejudice.[17]

There was strong reluctance to show any sympathy for America's partners in the war. In some quarters the thought that Britain had helped to lead the country from its course of peace made anti-British feeling all the more bitter. It was still widely believed that the press was being subsidized from London. According to George Seibel, a prominent German-American journalist, writing in the April number of the Alliance organ, "Congress ought to investigate how much British money is spent in this country to subsidize the hired liars of the Allied press propaganda." Herman Fellinger, president of the Cleveland Alliance, declared on April 14 that the German-Americans would not join in the intensive farm movement, because it would help Great Britain. "All German-Americans," he argued, with a logic that must have baffled many, "while they are backing America as against Germany,

[17] *Mitteilungen*, May, 1917, pp. 4, 8.

are praying for the defeat of Great Britain and her Allies. It is too much to expect them to raise foodstuffs for the Allies." The Central Alliance of Pennsylvania in July began to urge that only volunteers should be drafted for service outside the United States, and asked all its members to "inundate" the House Committee on Military Affairs with petitions in favor of the Mason bill, which had been introduced into Congress for that purpose.[18]

At the same time there was no inclination to condemn the war aims of the German government publicly, as some of the more violent German-baiting newspapers continually demanded. At the special meeting called by Weismann on April 8 the New York Alliance, while pledging its loyalty to the American cause, rejected a resolution placing the blame for the war upon Germany. The Illinois Alliance was equally explicit in its professions of loyalty at Chicago on April 28, but firmly declared that its members would not debase themselves to a mob of *Gesinnungslumpen* by joining in the general outcry against Germany and her allies. When, on July 26, the National Security League circularized certain German-American organizations for a definite condemnation of German war aims, Weismann replied that it was not for the German-Americans to act apart from the rest of the nation with reference to Germany. The Central Verein of Newark, New Jersey, on September 24, even drew up a protest to Congress against "the spread of slanderous stories" about German soldiers.[19]

Occasional displays of tactlessness provided opponents with an opportunity for impugning the loyalty of the Alliance. It made two such errors, in printing in its monthly organ questionable statements by irreconcilables. The first, published in May, was a report of a lecture delivered by Kuno Francke before the German Club of the University of Penn-

[18] *Ibid.*, April, 1917, p. 6; August, 1917, p. 8; *New York Times*, April 15, 1917.
[19] *New York Times*, April 9, July 28, September 25, 1917; *New-Yorker Staats-Zeitung*, April 28, 1917.

sylvania, in which it was stated that "even if the German arms—which fortunately is unlikely—should finally be overcome by a superiority in men and money, the German spirit will remain." The second was an article by Edmund von Mach, in the June issue, lamenting the change of front of the German-language press and the German-American organizations after the United States entered the war:

One almost died of shame when he saw this change of front here. One day Wilson was a terrible person because he wanted a war with Germany, the next he was a fine fellow because he had attained his desire, and out of fear of *lèse majesté* addresses of loyalty were sent to him. And that happened here in a country where one had pledged loyalty to the Constitution and no one else.

The German element has forfeited its every right if it now hides itself in cowardly fashion behind its citizenship papers, and denies the best that God has given it.[20]

Local Alliances sometimes found themselves at variance with the authorities. On November 8, 1917, the police banned the annual celebrations of the Alliance of Kansas City, Missouri, following remonstrance from the other residents. Missouri, indeed, seems to have been very much the center of trouble. In July three members of the executive committee of the State Alliance had been arrested in St. Louis. On April 13, 1918, the state president was prosecuted under Section 3 of the Espionage Act for stating in a newspaper interview that the war would be over in six months with Germany the victor. On January 25 the president of the Kansas Alliance was prosecuted under the same act, for statements in the *Missouri Staats-Zeitung*. "Of course," he was alleged to have written, "I realize that if the Kaiser conquers this country they will lose the chance to vote for a President who kept us out of war, only to plunge us in without any consultation of the people."[21]

[20] *Mitteilungen*, May, 1917, p. 1; June, 1917, p. 1.
[21] *New York Times*, November 9, 1917; April 14, 1918; *Mitteilungen*, August, 1917, p. 3; *Hearings on the German-American Alliance*, 636–637.

At the same time the support given to the Liberty Loan in other quarters indicated considerable enthusiasm for the American cause. John A. Schneiders of the Florida Alliance, which on April 5, 1917, had offered its new hundred-thousand-dollar clubhouse to the Red Cross, claimed to have sold eleven thousand dollars worth of Liberty Bonds. At the annual autumn festival of the Brooklyn Alliance, on October 14, Henry Weismann urged members to participate in the Loan as "a test of our usefulness as a patriotic American Alliance in a period of great national danger." So impressed was the *New York Times* that, after months of adverse comment, it had to admit that "members of the Alliance have seen a light." Pennsylvania made a particularly impressive effort. On October 22 the Allegheny County Alliance appropriated a thousand dollars from its membership fund for this purpose. By November 1 John B. Mayer of the Pennsylvania Central Alliance had sold over a hundred thousand dollars' worth of bonds. Returns from fifty German-American societies in the Pittsburgh area indicated that 1,394 members had purchased Liberty Bonds amounting to $217,250. When the second loan was floated, the Allegheny County Alliance subscribed $223,500 from its 1,457 members. This the Treasury Department acknowledged as "an irrefutable proof of patriotism and loyalty and a wise act of thrift."[22]

Constitutionally, the Alliance began to experience some difficult times after the United States entered the war. After August, 1914, it had increased considerably in numerical strength, claiming at the zenith of its power to represent forty-five state Alliances, with ten thousand affiliated German-American organizations and three million members. But after April, 1917, it began to decline rapidly. Hexamer endeavored to tighten up its organization by appointing a Committee for Ways and Means, with its seat at Indianapolis, to help with

[22] *Hearings on the German-American Alliance*, 184; *New York Times*, October 15, 18, 23, 1917; *Hearings on the German-American Alliance*, 398, 450, 571–572.

its government and also to be of service to its members who were victimized as a result of war prejudice. After April, *Mitteilungen* published few reports from the branches. In some quarters there was considerable dissatisfaction with the stand taken by the leaders, the New York Alliance experiencing in September an open revolt against the policy of Henry Weismann.[23]

The decision not to hold a national convention in 1917 was indicative of the debility brought upon the Alliance by the war. It was in striking contrast to the elaborate preparations and the ostentation which had accompanied the last national convention, at San Francisco in August, 1915. On May 5, 1917, Joseph Keller of Indiana and Leo Stern of Wisconsin both declared themselves against the idea of a convention. "When times have become more settled," it was said, "and men have freed themselves from their hysteria, then we can calmly proceed with the great work once more." To decide the question, a meeting of the executive committee and state presidents was summoned at Chicago on November 29. This was poorly attended, for two of the vice-presidents of the National Alliance had already resigned, and no delegates came from the far West. Illinois, Missouri, and Michigan were in favor of a convention, and a few violent speeches were made from these states with a view to arousing the other branches. "We must stand upon our constitutional rights . . . ," declared one delegate. "Submission, crawling on our knees will do us no good. Don't fear we shall make ourselves more obnoxious—we can't be more obnoxious than we are." The eastern delegates, however, were firm in their opposition, and as a result it was decided to have no national convention of the Alliance during the rest of the war.[24]

[23] *Mitteilungen*, September, 1915, p. 3; April, 1917, p. 8; August, 1917, p. 8. The up-state branches resented the attitude of the city Alliance in condemning Wilson. An emergency state convention was called on September 3, 1917, to settle some of the differences. *New York Times*, September 4, 1917.
[24] *Mitteilungen*, June, 1917, p. 8; *New York Times*, December 2, 1917.

Hexamer, whose health had not been good for some time, began gradually to recede from the leadership of the German-American movement. In May, 1917, he resigned from the presidency of the German Society of Pennsylvania, an office of some academic distinction which he had held for many years.[25] In the Alliance he ceased to exert the power which since 1899 had made him one of the most prominent men of German parentage in the country. His "strictly American position" after the severance of diplomatic relations with Germany was said to have aroused resentment among certain sections of his followers, and to have made further activity in the German-American cause "distasteful" to him.[26] On November 29, 1917, he resigned the leadership of the National Alliance, and recommended as his successor the Reverend Siegmund Georg von Bosse.[27]

Like Hexamer, Pastor von Bosse was an American by birth. Though only twenty-five years of age, he was an able speaker and writer both in German and in English, and had been secretary to the Chicago Conference Committee in 1916. In 1917 he was also president of the Delaware Alliance. On assuming office as president of the National Alliance, he made it his task to keep the organization together during the trying times which it was experiencing. This task he outlined as follows in his inaugural message of December 18:

In spite of all baiting, we shall not allow ourselves to be robbed of the belief that we, as sober citizens and conscious of our race, belong to the best in the nation. And just because of this it will be possible for us, after the war, to carry out our noble mission in helping heal the gaping wounds and trying to do away with misunderstandings on this side and the other . . .

It is hardly possible to lay down a program today. During

[25] *Mitteilungen,* June, 1917, p. 3.
[26] See the article from *Der Zeitgeist* quoted in *Mitteilungen,* November, 1917, p. 8.
[27] *Hearings on the German-American Alliance,* 499; von Bosse, *Ein Kampf um Glauben und Volkstum,* 253.

SIEGMUND G. VON BOSSE
President of the National German-American Alliance, 1917–1918

the period of the war we must simply try to maintain our Alliance.[28]

The Alliance found it impossible to isolate itself from the general virus against everything German. "Millions of our fellow Americans," admitted Henry Weismann on March 13, 1918, "are impatient of things Germanic, while the clash of arms is heard and our boys die in large numbers daily, killed by German bullets." Branches of the Alliance began to dissolve or to adopt another name. On January 24 the Kansas City Alliance became the American Citizenship Association. On March 17 the Toledo Alliance voted indefinite suspension. Many other branches, while desiring to preserve their identity, nevertheless decided to refrain from holding conventions and general meetings.

On January 16, 1918, Senator William Henry King of Utah introduced into Congress a bill to repeal the charter of the National Alliance. This became the signal for action against the Alliance throughout the country. On March 17 Senator Theodore Douglas Robinson, with the approval, it was stated, of his kinsman Colonel Roosevelt, introduced into the New York legislature a bill to repeal the charter of the state Alliance. He also sponsored a measure to eject members of the Alliance from the management of the Herkimer Memorial Homestead. In Milwaukee, at a meeting on March 22, the Wisconsin Loyalty Legion, an organization formed to "give voice to the militant loyalists of the state," demanded that "Congress revoke the charter of the so-called German-American Alliance and that the Federal Department of Justice take steps to punish all who have made such an Alliance a cloak to cover crimes against the country."[29]

On May 28 Warren G. Harding of Ohio read before the

[28] Singer's *Jahrbuch,* 1918, p. 397; *New York Times,* December 19, 1917. Carl Wittke (*German-Americans and the World War,* 167) writes: "The new president was American-born, which probably explains his election." In any case, however, the Alliance had never had a national president who was not American-born. (Hexamer was born in Philadelphia on March 9, 1862.)
[29] *New York Times,* January 17, 25, March 14, 18, 23, 1918.

United States Senate a series of resolutions passed by the Mayor's Advisory War Committee of Cleveland, demanding the rescission of the charter of 1907. On the same day Theodore Roosevelt, having just risen from his sickbed, delivered before the Republican State Convention of Maine the last of his fierce attacks upon the Alliance. He who was not wholeheartedly American, the colonel declared, was really "a traitor to America." There could be no such thing as "a fifty-fifty allegiance." The majority of Americans of German blood, he believed, were men of exemplary loyalty. "But the men of German blood who have tried to be both Germans and Americans are not Americans at all, but traitors to America and tools and servants of Germany against America. Organizations like the German-American Alliance have served Germany against America. Hereafter we must see that the melting pot really does not melt. There should be but one language in this country—the English." [30]

Following the introduction of Senator King's bill, a subcommittee of the Senate Committee on the Judiciary was appointed to consider the activities of the Alliance during the years of the European war. According to Mr. von Bosse, this investigation was welcomed by its officers as an opportunity to clear themselves of the charge of disloyalty which had so frequently been raised against them. Hearings were held between February 23 and April 13, 1918, with Senator King presiding. [31]

The investigation is significant mainly in that it illustrates the general intolerance of the times. From a purely judicial aspect its proceedings were characterized by a surprising amount of distortion and misapprehension of the German-American position. The Alliance made a very poor defense,

[30] *Congressional Record,* 65 Congress, 2 Session, 56:4182; *New York Times,* March 29, 1918.
[31] "The officers offered to testify at any time and even asked for a hearing." Mr. von Bosse to the writer, Philadelphia, October 6, 1937. The hearings are all reported in the *Hearings on the German-American Alliance.*

partly because of the duress under which its officials were
working and the inadequate time allowed them to prepare
their case. The best stand was made by Mr. von Bosse, who,
after all, had been in charge of the organization for only three
months. Adolph Timm, who had been secretary of the National Alliance since its very beginning, and who might have
been expected to answer most effectively for its conduct, made
a complete *volte face,* and later solicited employment in the
government secret service.

The investigation failed to differentiate properly between
evidence based upon the activities of the Alliance before the
United States entered the war and after. All was taken together as proof that it had violated its charter and that it was
un-American. Quotations from its monthly organ were de-
tached from their context and used against it. Evidence in
German was presented before the committee in large quantities, and yet some of its members were unable to understand
the language. One member even remarked, when such evidence was brought to his attention, "That does not mean anything to me, that being in German."

The principal witness against the Alliance was Gustavus
Ohlinger, who, as we have seen, had been a leading figure in
the campaign against the hyphen. The basis of his charges
was that the Alliance was identical in its plans and activities
with the Pan-German Union of Germany. "If allowed to
continue," he asserted, "if happily the war had not intervened
and aroused the people of the United States to the danger of
Pan-Germanism, the activities of this Alliance, if permitted
to continue, would have created a solid German bloc in the
population which could be used in favor of German policy,
and at the same time it would have resulted in disintegrating
the rest of the population so that there would have been
no national spirit in America whatever, and America would
have eventually simply fallen into the same position as
Austria-Hungary; it would have become a fief of the German

Empire." He then proceeded to trace the political activities of the Alliance, charging that its stand with reference to many candidates in 1916 was determined by their attitude toward Germany. Yet he admitted that ninety per cent of its political efforts were concerned with the question of prohibition— a figure which in itself would seem to have invalidated somewhat his argument that it was a Pan-German organization working in the interests of a foreign country.

A second witness against the Alliance was Henry C. Campbell, assistant editor of the *Milwaukee Journal*. While pressing equally strongly the charge of Pan-Germanism, he also described its attempts to control politics in Wisconsin. He argued that the part which the Alliance had taken in the election of 1916 was in contravention of its own constitution and of the laws of the United States under which it enjoyed its public charter. Other witnesses endeavored likewise to connect the organization with the Pan-German movement of Berlin, submitting excerpts from the writings of Bernhardi and others, and from the *Alldeutsche Blätter,* to prove that the Alliance had been welcomed as an instrument of German policy. Much was also made of the frequently misinterpreted German Delbrück Law of July, 1913, which was construed as permitting Germans in the United States to remain subjects of the *Reich* while taking out American citizenship papers.[32]

The investigation was accompanied by a running commentary of virulent abuse of the Alliance in the daily press. Its members were described as "spies and suspects"[33] and "the Kaiser's best friends";[34] the Alliance itself was a "nursery of alien disloyalty."[35] The investigation was wildly acclaimed as "scotching spy and sedition,"[36] "checking a cancerous

[32] *Hearings on the German-American Alliance*, 10–11, 61, 89, 95, 103 ff., 254, 649. *Alldeutsche Blätter* was the organ of the Pan-German Union (Alldeutscher Verband).

[33] *Elyria* [Ohio] *Telegram*, March 25, 1918. The writer is indebted to Mr. von Bosse for the use of press clippings from his scrapbook on this question.

[34] *Saturday Blade* (Chicago), March 16, 1918.

[35] *The Bee* (Omaha), April 1, 1918.   [36] *Boston News Bureau*, April 3, 1918.

growth,"[37] and "disbanding the Boche-Americans."[38] All sorts of threats were made against the Alliance leaders, and Mr. von Bosse found it advisable to leave Wilmington, Delaware, where he was pastor, until the furor subsided.[39]

The Senate subcommittee reported the King bill favorably, and on July 2, 1918, Congress repealed the act of 1907 which had granted a charter to the Alliance. The New York legislature had already, on April 10, passed the Robinson bill, with the assurance that "with this law on the statute books . . . we will never again have hyphenated organizations running amuck, sowing seeds of disloyalty among the people and attempting to make our public schools centers of German Kultur."[40]

The passage of the King bill, however, had been forestalled on April 11 by the action of the Alliance leaders themselves. Meeting in Philadelphia, the executive committee agreed to dissolve the national organization and to turn over its funds of twenty-six thousand dollars to the American Red Cross. The National German-American Alliance, it was announced, "hereby accepts the resignation of its President and all of its officials, closes its offices, and adjourns *sine die,* leaving it to the Congress of the United States, under a power reserved in the Act granting its charter, to revoke the same. As American citizens of German blood, whole-heartedly and without reservation, we say to our fellow citizens that together with them we shall ever stand ready to defend this Government and this country against all foes, internal and external, to the end that the liberty and freedom guaranteed by the Constitution shall forever prevail."[41]

With that statement, which was communicated to the press on the next day, it brought to a close its seventeen years' activity in the German-American cause.

[37] *Standard-Union* (Brooklyn), April 12, 1918.
[38] *Jacksonville* [Florida] *Metropolis,* April 12, 1918.
[39] Statement to the writer, Philadelphia, October 6, 1937.
[40] *New York Times,* April 11, 1918.   [41] *Ibid.,* April 13, 1918.

IX

CONCLUSION

THE ABUSE THAT ACCOMPANIED THE DISSOLUTION OF THE AL-
liance in the spring of 1918 was but a more violent expression
of the general hostility that had dogged its activities ever
since August, 1914. Its opponents had always been many and
powerful. Throughout the European war it had been faced
with the combined antipathy of the Allied propagandists, the
pro-Ally element in the American press and public life, the
Wilson administration and its friends, and thousands of
others who considered themselves just plain Americans and
who, stirred by the general campaign against hyphenism and
disloyalty, somehow felt the Alliance to be incompatible with
the best interests and traditions of this country.

The bad odor that sometimes attached itself to its name
was not entirely the result of British propaganda, or of American subservience to British culture and ideals, as was constantly argued by the German-language press. While there
was much in its very nature that would be applauded by other
Americans, there was also much that might be resented. To
many whose ancestors had rejected George III, it did seem
perhaps incongruous that certain German-Americans should
attempt to reconcile with their devotion to American liberty
and republican democracy an admiration for Kaiser William
II—or any other representative of the German nation. And
when these German-Americans proceeded to preach to native
citizens on the nature of true Americanism (however sincere
their motives),[1] and used purely German celebrations, such
as the Bismarck Centenary of April, 1915, to denounce the

[1] See, for example, the editorial, "Is Ours an American Government?" in
the *Illinois Staats-Zeitung* (Chicago), October 21, 1915.

174

"pro-British policy" of the American government, to many
their actions must have bordered upon presumption.[2]

Some Alliance leaders appear to have had a weakness for
impressing people adversely. Their tone and manner, which
to the German mind might have meant something far different, by the unenlightened might have been taken for arro-
gance and bombast. "The Allies could not have wished for
any better confederates," declared the Socialist *New Yorker
Volkszeitung* on May 8, 1915, in an article denouncing their
"reserve-lieutenant tone" and "ostentatious inaptitude" as
the cause of German-American unpopularity.[3] In their methods they were not always consistent. In demanding "strict
American neutrality" (when logic and every just human right
seemed to be on their side) they often could not resist deco-
rating their meetings with the flags of Germany and con-
cluding their speeches to the strains of *Deutschland über
Alles* and *Die Wacht am Rhein*.[4] They objected to the use of
American money by the Allies in the form of loans, but exported large sums themselves for German war relief, and permitted their newspapers to help the sale of German bonds.

Capable as he was as a leader of men, Hexamer would not
always seem to have been a master of tact. On more than one
occasion an error of judgment on his part brought unnecessary abuse upon the Alliance. At one time, for example, he
allowed postcards to be made for sale in the United States,
with a picture of himself between the German and Austrian
emperors—thus giving his opponents further cause to insinu-
ate that he regarded himself as a sort of imperial viceroy.[5]
On March 23, 1916, he used the occasion of a visit to the

---

[2] See *Mitteilungen*, May, 1915, p. 1; Singer's *Jahrbuch*, 1916, p. 38.

[3] For a further discussion of German-American unpopularity after August,
1914, see Singer's *Jahrbuch*, 1916, p. 92.

[4] See the reports of meetings in *Mitteilungen*, January, 1915, p. 18, and
March, 1915, p. 23; *Westliche Post*, January 11, 1915.

[5] In the opinion of one German-American writer, this action of Hexamer's
"grenzte an ein politisches Schildbürgerstückchen" and was "ein Symbol der
allgemeinen Ungeschlicklichkeit . . . der Deutschamerikaner." *New Yorker
Kampf um Wahrheit und Frieden*, 31.

office of Edwin Lowry Humes, United States attorney for the western district of Pennsylvania, to attack the American republican form of government, saying—to the utter surprise of those present—that he considered a constitutional monarchy preferable.[6] Phrases in his speeches also lent themselves at times to misrepresentation, as, for example, in November, 1915, when he told a Milwaukee audience that he was against the rapid assimilation of the German-Americans into the general American population, on the ground that they would never "be prepared to descend to the level of an inferior culture."[7]

Although the Alliance was by far the largest organization of any one racial group in American history, considerable sections of the German element held rigidly aloof. According to J. Otto Pfeiffer, editor of the St. Louis *Westliche Post,* there was constant tension between the Alliance and the German Catholics, whom it frequently regarded with contempt as *Kirchen Deutsche.*[8] Many German-American groups, who merely favored organization of a social nature, felt that they had no place inside the Alliance, on account of its immersion in local politics. Throughout the war, and despite some efforts at cooperation on the peace question, the Alliance had to face the fierce opposition of the German-American Socialists. The latter regarded the war as a war of imperialism, in which Germany was as culpable as the rest of the European Powers, and denounced the activities of the German-American leaders—in the words of the *New Yorker Volkszeitung*—as "patriotic lunacy."[9]

In its leadership, and largely in its aims, the Alliance was

[6] *Hearings on the German-American Alliance,* 115, 309.
[7] Hermann Hagedorn, *Where Do You Stand? An Appeal to Americans of German Origin* (Macmillan, New York, 1918), 44–45; *Mitteilungen,* January, 1916, p. 6; *Germania-Herold,* December 7, 1915.
[8] Statement to the writer, St. Louis, December 29, 1937.
[9] *New Yorker Volkszeitung,* May 8, 1915. In 1914 the German-American Socialists had quite a flourishing German-language press, with a circulation of some 126,900. This included two daily and ten weekly newspapers. Ayer's *Newspaper Annual and Directory,* 1914, pp. 1253–1258.

essentially a middle-class organization. Its officers were mainly newspaper editors, college professors, clergymen, or independent business men. Hexamer was a prosperous engineer; John B. Mayer a Philadelphia court reporter; Joseph Keller owned a textile business at Indianapolis; Adolph Timm was a journalist; Theodore Sutro a well-to-do New York lawyer; Leo Stern a supervisor of schools. Testimony before the Senate subcommittee on March 2, 1918, revealed something of the status of other prominent members:

Cuno H. Rudolph . . . Chairman of the Board of Commissioners of the District of Columbia . . . Mr. Pagenstecher is one of the greatest merchants of the country. Mr. Hasslacher is one of the greatest chemists of the country. Mr. Erbslöh is one of the greatest importers in New York. Dr. Hugo Schweitzer . . . was known in all European countries as one of the greatest chemists in the world. Dr. Stadtmueller is one of the best known physicians in New York . . . John Schwaab is one of the judges in Ohio; Blankenburg was Mayor of Philadelphia. . . . There is William Knauth, the well-known banker, Lindemann, a well-known engineer, and so forth. . . .[10]

In Germany, the real nature and aims of the Alliance, in so far as they were known at all, were never properly understood. Absurd comments upon its activities in the German press, and extravagant claims as to its political power, managed to do considerable harm when they found their way (often via London) into the United States.[11] Typical of the German viewpoint was Karl Jünger's *Deutsch-Amerika mobil!* which was written with the object of enlightening people in Germany upon the nature and aspirations of the various German-American movements. In this book, Jünger en-

---

[10] *Hearings on the German-American Alliance,* 143. For further information regarding the social status of leaders of the Alliance, see Heinrici, *Das Buch der Deutschen,* 801 ff.

[11] See, for example, the comments of the *Rheinisch-Westfalische Zeitung,* the *Frankfurter Zeitung,* and the *Berliner Tageblatt* on the Washington conference of January 30, 1915, quoted in the *Literary Digest,* 50:301, 361 (February 13, 20, 1915); and the *New York Times,* February 8, 1915.

deavored also to offer certain suggestions as to how the German-Americans might make themselves effective in American public life. His advice seemed almost to assume an official aspect when Admiral Knorr, of the German Naval Service, honored it with a preface. The German-Americans, in his opinion, should constantly play up the Japanese danger to convince their fellow citizens of the folly of sympathizing with the Allies. They should also point out the advantages that might accrue from the annexation of Canada, and, failing to arouse enthusiasm for this project, they might cooperate with German reservists here in an invasion of that country.[12] In view of such wild suggestions, it was not exactly surprising that certain pro-Ally newspapers were able to misrepresent the German-Americans, along with von Papen, Boy-Ed, Rintelen, and others, as conspirators in the German cause.[13]

The universal insistence upon the use of the German language became something of a handicap to the Alliance in the war years. It robbed its propaganda of much of the subtlety that was characteristic of its pro-Ally opponents. There was, in fact, some contradiction between the use of German and the attempts of German-American leaders to exert an influence in American public affairs. By constantly using German as their medium of expression, they seemed to disable themselves from winning the general sympathy of their fellow citizens. For, to the majority of Americans, German was after all a foreign language. And when the German-Americans clung to it so tenaciously they inevitably gave the impression that they had more in common with Germany than with America.

One can readily appreciate the sentiments of German-born Americans in desiring that their children grow up with an ability to speak the language of their European forbears. Yet the mere fact that German happened to be the ancestral lan-

[12] Karl Jünger, *Deutsch-Amerika mobil!* mit einem Geleitwort von Exzellenz von Knorr, Admiral z. D. (Behrs Verlag, Berlin, 1915), 139–141.
[13] For rumors of German-American plans to invade Canada, see *Mitteilungen,* February, 1915, p. 22.

guage of many American citizens was no sound reason for the rest of Americans why it should be taught, second to English, in the public schools. It could be demonstrated that this did not necessarily enrich the United States to any greater degree with the cultural treasures of Germany, for some of the most devoted scholars of German culture and literature in the United States have been men who could boast of no German ancestry. And, in any case, the second generation of German-Americans tended to grow up culturally and politically American, and not German. Unless their parents were able to send them back to the fatherland to rejoin relatives or complete their education, Germany remained for them a foreign country. And there was no very obvious indication on their part that they regretted the fact. Some few of them might still consider themselves with pride as Germans, but many more were thankful to be just Americans.[14]

In its inception, the National German-American Alliance could justly claim that it had a real purpose to fulfil: the purpose of educating Germans in the ways of America, and, at the same time, of helping native Americans to appreciate and understand their new countrymen of German origin. Other institutions, however, many of them of a public nature, were quite capable of serving this need, without the disadvantage of segregating the Germans from the rest of the immigrant population. Thus to some Americans it would be hard to justify an organization, like the Alliance, which followed along racial lines. Some might doubt the right of the German-Americans, or any other group, to cling so tenaciously in culture and sympathy to their native country, and further to express a certain admiration for its leaders and form of government. Some might even question the propriety of any foreign-born element drawing apart from the rest of the population, when America itself had a real claim to nationhood.

[14] "In fact," adds Mr. von Bosse, "many were outspokenly anti-German."

BIBLIOGRAPHY

CONTEMPORARY SOURCES

It has not been possible to consult any collections of private papers in the preparation of this work, for the reason that none have yet been made available for historical purposes. But the writer has been in correspondence with many prominent German-Americans and other leaders of the period who are still living, and information supplied by them has been used in the text. The following have been mentioned by name: Mr. Siegmund Georg von Bosse, former president of the German-American Alliance; Professor William Macneile Dixon, formerly of the British Department of Information; and the former Kaiser Wilhelm II, represented by the Generalverwaltung des vormaligen Preussischen Königshauses, of Berlin. Others have supplied information and strengthened the writer in some of his conclusions, but have requested that their correspondence be treated as private. The writer has also interveiwed such prominent German-Americans as Mr. von Bosse; Dr. Max Heinrici, head of the press bureau of the Alliance; and Mr. J. Otto Pfeiffer, editor of the St. Louis *Westliche Post*.

Much of the primary source material has been found in the reports of the various branches of the Alliance, published in *Mitteilungen des Deutschamerikanischen Nationalbundes der Vereinigten Staaten von Amerika; Bulletin of the National German-American Alliance* (Philadelphia, 1909–1918), complete files of which are to be found in the New York Public Library and in the library of the German Society of Pennsylvania, Philadelphia; also in the following German-language newspapers, files of which have been available (usually in complete form) at the places mentioned:

Cincinnatier Freie Presse, 1914–1918. Publishers, Cincinnati.
Germania-Herold (Milwaukee), 1914–1918. Wisconsin State Historical Library.

Illinois Staats-Zeitung (Chicago), 1914–1918. Incomplete file, Chicago Public Library.

Milwaukee-Sonntagspost, 1914–1918. Sunday edition of the *Germania-Herold.* Wisconsin State Historical Library.

Mississippi Blätter (St. Louis), 1914–1918. Sunday edition of the *Westliche Post.* Publishers, St. Louis.

New-Yorker Staats-Zeitung, 1914–1918. Library of Congress.

New Yorker Volkszeitung (Socialist), 1914–1918. Wisconsin State Historical Library.

Volksblatt und Freiheits-Freund (Pittsburgh), 1914–1918. Carnegie Library, Pittsburgh.

Der Westen (Chicago). Sunday edition of the *Illinois Staats-Zeitung* to August, 1915. Chicago Public Library.

Westliche Post (St. Louis), 1914–1918. Publishers, St. Louis.

OTHER NEWSPAPERS AND PERIODICALS

Americana Germanica (New York), 1899–1903.

American Review of Reviews, 1914–1917.

Atlantic Monthly, 1914–1917.

Deutsche Geschichtsforschung für Missouri, 1913–1914.

The Fatherland (New York), 1914–1917.

German-American Annals (New York), 1903–1917.

The Independent, 1914–1917.

Literary Digest, 1914–1918.

Living Age, 1914–1917.

Milwaukee Sentinel, 1914–1917.

The Nation, 1914–1917.

New York Times, 1914–1918.

New Republic, 1914–1917.

The Outlook, 1914–1917.

Providence Journal, 1914–1917.

World (New York), 1914–1917.

GOVERNMENT PUBLICATIONS

Brewing and Liquor Interests and German Propaganda: Hearings before a Subcommittee of the Committee on the Judiciary, United States Senate, 65 Congress, 2 Session. Washington, 1919.

Congressional Record, 1914–1917.

Correspondence between the Secretary of State and the Chairman of the Committee on Foreign Relations. 65 Congress, 3 Session, Senate Document no. 716. Washington, 1915.

Exportations of Munitions of War: Hearings on H. J. Res. 377 and 378, House Committee on Foreign Affairs, 63 Congress, 3 Session. Washington, 1915.

Munitions Industry, Report on Existing Legislation, by a special committee on investigation of the munitions industry, United States Senate, pursuant to S. Res. 206. 74 Congress, 2 Session, Senate Report no. 944, Part 5. Washington, 1936.

National German-American Alliance: Hearings before the Subcommittee of the Committee on the Judiciary, United States Senate, 65 Congress, 2 Session, on S. 3529. Washington, 1918. Cited as *Hearings on the German-American Alliance.*

Thirteenth Census of the United States, 1910, Vol. 1.

GENERAL WORKS

America and the War. Letters and comments written for publication in the press. Printed by Maurice Leon, New York. 1915.

American Newspaper Annual and Directory. Ayer, Philadelphia. 1914.

BAILEY, THOMAS A. "The Sinking of the Lusitania." *American Historical Review,* 41:54–74 (October, 1935).

BAKER, RAY S., and DODD, WILLIAM E., eds. *The Public Papers of Woodrow Wilson: The New Democracy.* 2 vols. Harper, New York. 1926.

BARTHOLDT, RICHARD. *From Steerage to Congress.* Dorrance, Philadelphia. 1931.

BERNSTORFF, JOHANN H. VON. *My Three Years in America.* Skeffington, London. 1920.

BOSSE, GEORG VON. *Ein Kampf um Glauben und Volkstum.* Belsersche Verlag, Stuttgart. 1920.

BRYAN, WILLIAM J. and MARY B. *Memoirs of William Jennings Bryan.* Winston, Chicago. 1925.

BÜLOW, BERNHARD VON. *Memoirs.* Little, Brown, Boston. 1931.

CHERADAME, ANDRÉ. *The United States and Pan-Germania.* Scribners, New York. 1918.

COLVIN, LEIGH. *Prohibition in the United States.* Doran, New York. 1926.

Democratic Text-Book. Democratic National Committee. 1916.

Deutsch-Amerikanisches Vereins-Adressbuch. German-American
Publishing Co., Milwaukee. 1914.

FAUST, ALBERT B. *The German Element in the United States.*
New edition. 2 vols. Steuben Society, New York. 1927.

GOEBEL, JULIUS. *Der Kampf um deutsche Kultur in Amerika.*
Leipzig. 1914.

HAGEDORN, HERMANN. *Where Do You Stand? An Appeal to
Americans of German Origin.* Macmillan, New York. 1918.

HEATON, JOHN L. *Cobb of "The World."* Dutton, New York.
1924.

HEINRICI, MAX, ed. *Das Buch der Deutschen in Amerika.* National German-American Alliance, Philadelphia. 1909.

HERRICK, GENEVIEVE F. and JOHN. *Life of William Jennings
Bryan.* Stanton, Chicago. 1925.

Im Kampfe für Wahrheit und Recht (pamphlet). German-
American Literary Defense Committee, New York. 1915.

JÜNGER, KARL. *Deutsch-Amerika mobil!* Behrs Verlag, Berlin.
1915.

KOELBLE, ALPHONSE G. *An Open Letter to the President of the
United States* (pamphlet). Koelble, New York. 1915.

LANSING, ROBERT. *War Memoirs.* Bobbs-Merrill, Indianapolis
and New York. 1935.

MILLIS, WALTER. *Road to War.* Houghton Mifflin, Boston.
1935.

OHLINGER, GUSTAVUS. *The German Conspiracy in American
Education.* Doran, New York. 1919.

———. *Their True Faith and Allegiance.* Macmillan, New York.
1916.

OLDS, FRANK P. "'Kultur' in American Politics." *Atlantic
Monthly,* 108: 382–391 (September, 1916).

O'LEARY, JEREMIAH. *My Political Trial and Experiences.* Jefferson Publishing Co., New York. 1919.

PAXSON, FREDERIC L. *Pre-War Years, 1913–1917.* Houghton Mifflin, Boston. 1936.

Republican Campaign Text-Book. Republican National Committee. 1916.

ROTHENFELDER, FRANZ, ed. *New Yorker Kampf um Wahrheit*

und Frieden, aus den Kriegserinnerungen eines Deutsch-amerikaners. Augsburg. 1917.

ROUQUETTE, LOUIS. *La Propagande germanique aux États-Unis.* Chapelot, Paris. 1918.

Selections from the Correspondence of Theodore Roosevelt and Henry Cabot Lodge, 1884–1918. 2 vols. Scribners, New York. 1925.

SEYMOUR, CHARLES. *American Neutrality, 1914–1917.* Yale University Press, New Haven. 1935.

——, ed. *The Intimate Papers of Colonel House,* vols. 1 and 2. Houghton Mifflin, Boston. 1925, 1928.

SINGER, MICHAEL. *Jahrbuch der Deutschen in Chicago.* Singer, Chicago. Published annually, 1914–1918.

SKAGGS, WILLIAM. *German Conspiracies in America.* Fisher Unwin, London. 1915.

SQUIRES, JAMES D. *British Propaganda at Home and in the United States from 1914 to 1917.* Harvard Historical Monographs, no. 6. Harvard University Press, Cambridge. 1935.

SULLIVAN, MARK. *Our Times, the United States, 1900–1925.* Scribners, New York. 1926–1935. Vol. 5, *Over Here.*

THAYER, WILLIAM R. *Life and Letters of John Hay.* 2 vols. Houghton Mifflin, New York. 1915.

TUMULTY, JOSEPH P. *Woodrow Wilson as I Know Him.* Published by the *Literary Digest.* 1921.

VIERECK, GEORGE S. *Spreading Germs of Hate.* Liveright, New York. 1930.

——. *The Strangest Friendship in History: Woodrow Wilson and E. M. House.* Liveright, New York. 1932.

VOSS, ERNST. *Vier Jahrzehnte in Amerika.* Deutsche Verlagsanstalt, Stuttgart. 1929.

WILE, FREDERIC W. *The German-American Plot.* Pearson, London. 1915.

WITTKE, CARL. *German-Americans and the World War. Ohio Historical Collections,* vol. 5. Ohio State Archaeological and Historical Society, Columbus. 1936.

INDEX

Abendpost (Chicago), 119
Alldeutsche Blätter, 20, 172
Allegheny County (Pennsylvania), German-American Alliance of, 16, 118, 132, 156, 166
Alliance, *see* National German-American Alliance
Allied loans, extent of, 155
American Independence Conference, 142n
American Independence Union, 53, 81n, 133
American Neutrality League, 98
American Truth Society, 7, 61n
Ancient Order of Hibernians, 6
Andreae, Percy, 14, 15, 17, 18, 128
Anti-Saloon League, 10–11, 12, 17
Atlantic Monthly, 102, 103
Austro-Hungarian embassy, 44n

Bartholdt, Richard, bill to prohibit munitions trade, 48–50, 52–57, 62n; and *Lusitania* crisis, 70; attempts to make German-American influence felt in election of *1916,* 103, 112, 116, 146; controversy with Maurice Leon, 105; mentioned, 5, 30n, 32, 47, 76, 88
Bazaars, for German war relief, 38
Bente, Friedrich, 126
Berkemeier, Reverend G. C., 52, 82, 133
Bernstorff, Count Johann Heinrich von, 10, 22, 67, 139, 143, 152
Blacklist, British, of German-American firms, 135–136, 155
Blockade, German-American attempts to circumvent, 38–39
Bloedel, H. C., fights against prohibition, 16; war relief work, 35; denounces Wilson, 80
Bonheur, Lucien, 139

Bosse, Reverend Georg von, 51n
Bosse, Reverend Siegmund Georg von, on National German-American Alliance and prohibition, 11n; and election of *1916,* 123, 126, 136, 151n; president of National German-American Alliance, 168–169, 170–171, 173
Boston, German-American Alliance of, 26
Brand, Horace L., 52, 65
Brandt, Louis E., 132n
Brewers, subsidizing National German-American Alliance, 14
British propaganda in the United States, accusations against German-Americans, 86, 98–102; demand for investigation of, 163
Brooklyn, German-American Alliance of, 13
Brooklyn Eagle, 53
Brooks, Sydney, 100
Bruncken, Ernst, 40, 104
Bryan, William Jennings, and munitions trade, 56; German-American attitude toward, 73; resignation and rapprochement with German-Americans, 74–78, 82, 87, 89, 95, 136
Buchanan, Frank, 76
Bulletin of National German-American Alliance, *see Mitteilungen*
Bülow, Prince Bernhard von, 2n
Burgess, John W., 28

California, German-American Alliance of, and election of *1916,* 118, 132
Call, Homer D., 81
Campbell, Henry C., 172
Canada, Germans of, 8
Canton (Ohio), German-American Alliance of, 152

DATE DUE

10/30			